ARE YOU NOW OR
HAVE YOU EVER BEEN

Also by Eric Bentley

AUTHOR OF:

A CENTURY OF HERO-
    WORSHIP
THE PLAYWRIGHT AS
    THINKER
BERNARD SHAW
IN SEARCH OF THEATRE
THE DRAMATIC EVENT

WHAT IS THEATRE?
THE LIFE OF THE DRAMA
THE THEATRE OF COMMITMENT
A TIME TO DIE
THE RED WHITE AND BLACK
THE RECANTATION OF
    GALILEO GALILEI
THEATRE OF WAR

EDITOR OF:

THE IMPORTANCE OF
    SCRUTINY
FROM THE MODERN
    REPERTOIRE (*three
    volumes*)
THE PLAY
THE MODERN THEATRE
    (*six volumes*)
THE CLASSIC THEATRE
    (*four volumes*)
LET'S GET A DIVORCE

THE THEORY OF THE
    MODERN STAGE
SHAW ON MUSIC
THE WORKS OF BERTOLT BRECHT
THE STORM OVER THE DEPUTY
THE BRECHT-EISLER SONG BOOK
THE GREAT PLAYWRIGHTS
THIRTY YEARS OF TREASON
THE GENIUS OF THE
    ITALIAN THEATRE

TRANSLATOR:

twelve plays of Brecht, five plays of Pirandello,
FILUMENA MARTURANO *by Eduardo de Filippo,*
THE WIRE HARP *by Wolf Biermann,* and other items

*Eric Bentley is heard, as either reader or singer,
on the following record albums:*

BENTLEY ON BRECHT
BRECHT BEFORE THE UN-
    AMERICAN ACTIVITIES
    COMMITTEE
SONGS OF HANNS EISLER

THE EXCEPTION AND THE
    RULE
A MAN'S A MAN
THE ELEPHANT CALF
BENTLEY ON BIERMANN
THE QUEEN OF 42ND STREET

The Investigation of
Show Business by the Un-American
Activities Committee 1947–1958

ARE YOU NOW OR
HAVE YOU EVER BEEN

Eric Bentley

HARPER COLOPHON BOOKS
HARPER & ROW, PUBLISHERS
New York, Evanston, San Francisco, London

ARE YOU NOW OR HAVE YOU EVER BEEN: THE INVESTIGATION OF
SHOW BUSINESS BY THE UN-AMERICAN ACTIVITIES COMMITTEE,
1947–1958. Copyright © 1972 by Eric Bentley.

First HARPER COLOPHON edition published 1972.

LIBRARY OF CONGRESS CATALOG CARD NUMBER: 72–76979

STANDARD BOOK NUMBER: 06–0910062

For Philip and Daniel Berrigan

Preface

The dialogue of *Are You Now or Have You Ever Been* is taken from hearings before the Un-American Activities Committee. Hence no resemblance between the witness and the actual person is coincidental. These characters wrote their own lines into the pages of history. Though I did abridge and tidy up the record, I did not write in additional dialogue. Transpositions—of words within a sentence or of sentences within a sequence—I tried to hold down to a minimum lest there be any distortion of the sense.

No names have been changed, except that names of Committee members occur only as mentioned in the dialogue. Committee membership varied a good deal in the course of the eleven years covered. Since these variations are unimportant to the action here presented, Committee members are designated in the text by number (CM 1, CM 2, etc.); the Chairman, also not the same man throughout the period, is called *the* Chairman; the Investigators are called Investigator, 2nd Investigator, etc. The image is of a single Committee in session throughout, presided over by a single Chairman, assisted by Investigators. Confronting them is a witness, usually accompanied by his attorney. All participants are equipped with microphones.* The room was not

---

* The *New York Times* described the Hollywood hearings of 1947 as follows: "Scores of correspondents covered the proceedings, which took place before 30 microphones, six newsreel cameras and blazing klieg lights. Fervent applause, boos, cheers, hisses and laughter punctuated the packed sessions, at which Mr. [J. Parnell] Thomas presided with a rapping gavel and flourishes of rhetoric."

always the same. It was not always even in Washington, D.C. But, for the imagination, a single room will suffice, looking like any courtroom, or, better, like any larger room in a Government building. Except as the text itself indicates that the room is cleared for an "executive" or closed session, there is an audience, and sometimes it fills the room to overflowing and the Chairman has to pound his gavel for attention. When the witness is a movie star, the Chairman may have to ask press photographers to be less obtrusive. Sometimes a witness may himself object to the use of TV lights and cameras. Such is the transaction—the drama—known as Investigation.

The investigation of show business is presented here in the testimony of a small minority of those actually investigated, and this testimony has been abridged, edited, and arranged. (By "arrangement" I refer chiefly to the order in which the "scenes" are presented. This order—with a couple of tiny exceptions—is chronological, and yet chronology did not do my work for me: although after 1951 would come 1952, the question what to choose from the 1952 record was a matter of which 1952 items would follow upon the 1951 items with most "drama." It is by "arrangement" that the overall shape of the work is arrived at. It is by "arrangement" that the principal shock effect of this work—juxtaposition, collage—is produced.) All these processes—choice of witness, abridgment, editing, arrangement—bring into play the personal judgment, not to mention talent, of the writer responsible. To the extent that he is either a knave or a fool, the result will reflect his knavery or folly. I can only say I am aware of this, and I invite the skeptical or suspicious reader to check out his doubts and suspicions. Unlike many historians I am not using sources which the average person wouldn't have access to. On the contrary, I have used a record published by the United States Govern-

J. Parnell Thomas (*Acme Photo*).

J. Parnell Thomas, Bartley C. Crum, Robert W. Kenny,
Robert E. Stripling (*Acme Photo*).

John McDowell, Robert E. Stripling, Karl Mundt, J. Parnell Thomas, F. Edward Hebert (*Acme Photo*).

Herbert Biberman (*UPI*).

Lester Cole (*Acme Photo*).

Ring Lardner, Jr.
(*Acme Photo*).

Samuel Ornitz (*UPI*).

Adrian Scott (*UPI*).

Dalton Trumbo (*Acme Photo*).

John Howard Lawson
(*Acme Photo*).

Edward Dmytryk (*Acme Photo*).

Alvah Bessie (*Acme Photo*).

Albert Maltz (*Acme Photo*).

Seven of the Hollywood Ten: Samuel Ornitz, Ring Lardner, Jr., Albert Maltz, Alvah Bessie, Lester Cole, Herbert Biberman, Edward Dmytryk (*Acme Photo*).

Nine of the Hollywood Ten: Robert Scott, Edward Dmytryk, Samuel Ornitz, Lester Cole, Herbert Biberman, Albert Maltz, Alvah Bessie, John Lawson, Ring Lardner, Jr. (*Acme Photo*).

ment, and most of the testimony drawn upon can be found in its broader context in my own volume *Thirty Years of Treason*.

While I have my own opinions and commitments, I have tried to be fair, and my aim in employing a high degree of selectivity was not, lawyer-fashion, to make an overwhelming case for a client. The kind of client *I* represent would not be served by suppression of any relevant factors. Those who wish to study the investigation of show business in a more scholarly manner can do so by turning to my longer book or even to HUAC records as printed *in extenso* by the government. What I hope to have captured in this shorter treatment is a story, a newspaperman's "story," and a writer's, even perhaps a playwright's story: a dramatic action. I have succeeded for you, the reader, if the reading of this book holds you from beginning to end and leaves with you an impression of wholeness, of a single tale told at the proper pace in proper sequence, without waste motion, without loose ends.

Like almost anyone who tells a story, I would like to believe that I have also presented credible and interesting human beings. Some of the characters in *Are You Now or Have You Ever Been* pass too quickly across our line of vision to be portraits in any detail, but several of the witnesses whom the Committee held on to for hours (though here reduced to minutes) revealed themselves abundantly, more abundantly, in some instances, than they'd have wanted.

Lionel Stander's appearance before the Committee would repay study by dramatic critics. "Role playing!" said one of my friends who read the testimony. But Stander is by profession an actor, and what an actor does is play roles. An actor plays Georges Danton, let us say, making a speech when his life is at stake, when his every word and gesture is a matter of life and death. For Danton, not for the actor. Before the Committee, we find Lionel Stander *playing* with the idea of his life being at stake. It wasn't. No guillotine stood ready to cut off his head. The comic tone well expresses Stander's appreciation of this. Yet his life was, too, at stake: the Committee's target was a person's *livelihood,* his *living,* that without which he cannot live. Stander fought for his life like a tiger cat, yet it was less his own life he fought for—though blacklisted, he always maintained himself at a handsome level of income—than the lives of others and the principle of the thing. "Role playing," then. "Just putting on an act." "Song and dance." Call this, in sum, a benefit performance, for the benefit of his profession, especially its most victimized members, carried off with brio, "for the hell of it." The histrionic element in Stander's testimony I see, not as falsifying it, but as giving it style and form and, ultimately, the exact emphasis and significance which it required.

Students of the theatre will note that, while some witnesses offered only *monologue,* and at that *read* from a piece of paper, Stander at every point related himself to his audience, to both his audiences, the one physically present and, beyond that, the American people at such time as they would pay attention. He "bore witness" in constant interaction with Chairman and Investigator and Committee members, taunting them, shocking them, amusing them, dismaying them—and, finally, outplaying them. And although his prose is his own, as much as any monologue could be it is a prose of agile repartee, of fierce retort. Even what might strike his enemies as insincerity is part of the performance. Spontaneity is offset by control. Any apparent uncontrol is really controlled, as in all good theatre. Which again is only to say that Stander's encounter with the Committee is not mere experience but experience worked up into performance. And, if not a performance *for* his life, the performance, I would suspect, *of* his life.

Nor is Lionel Stander the only one whose nature, whose humanity is revealed here, and this by the traditional means of the drama: a human crisis brought to a head by a conflict among a few persons on a "stage" before an audience and expressed in passionate words.

January 1972

E.B.

This Committee is the grand jury of America. . . . What this Committee is trying to do is save the country.
—Congressman John E. Rankin, 1947, 1948

We have the problem of determining in this country the fine point where legitimate dissent ends and criminal disobedience begins.
—Congressman Richard H. Ichord, 1968

Eighteen Witnesses

Sam G. Wood

Edward Dmytryk

Ring Lardner, Jr.

Larry Parks

Sterling Hayden

José Ferrer

Abe Burrows

Elia Kazan

Tony Kraber

Jerome Robbins

Elliott Sullivan

Martin Berkeley

Lillian Hellman

Marc Lawrence

Lionel Stander

Zero Mostel

Arthur Miller

Paul Robeson

Part One

Are you now, or have you ever been, a member of the Communist Party? In 1947 the Un-American Activities Committee put this question to "the Hollywood Ten," a group of screen writers and screen directors who refused to testify, invoked the First Amendment, and, three years later, landed in jail for contempt of Congress. The Committee's adviser in this field was the Motion Picture Alliance for the Preservation of American Ideals.

INVESTIGATOR. Will you state your name?

MR. WOOD. Sam G. Wood.

INVESTIGATOR. What is your present occupation?

MR. WOOD. Motion picture producer and director.

INVESTIGATOR. Would you name to the Committee some of the films you have produced and directed?

MR. WOOD. *Goodbye Mr. Chips, Kitty Foyle, For Whom the Bell Tolls.* . . .

INVESTIGATOR. Mr. Wood, are you a member of the Motion Picture Alliance for the Preservation of American Ideals?

MR. WOOD. I am. I was its first president.

INVESTIGATOR. Will you tell the Committee why it was founded?

MR. WOOD. We felt that there was a definite effort by Communist Party members to take over the unions and guilds.

Sam G. Wood (*Acme Photo*).

Robert E. Stripling and John E. Rankin (*Acme Photo*).

INVESTIGATOR. Will you tell the Committee of the efforts of the Communists to infiltrate the Screen Directors Guild?

MR. WOOD. Our most serious time was when George Stevens, who was president, went into the service, and the Guild was turned over to John Cromwell. With the assistance of three or four others, Cromwell tried to steer us into the Red river.

INVESTIGATOR. Will you name the others?

MR. WOOD. Irving Pichel, Frank Tuttle, Edward Dmytryk. . . .

INVESTIGATOR. Mr. Wood, do the Communists maintain schools or laboratories in Hollywood for the purpose of training actors or writers?

MR. WOOD. They have a laboratory theater there.

INVESTIGATOR. What is the function of this?

MR. WOOD. The youngsters go to these schools, they get parts, they study, and we see them in theaters. The Laboratory Theater, I think, is definitely under the control of the Communist Party. Any kid that goes in there with American ideals hasn't a chance in the world. Then we have the Educational Center—

INVESTIGATOR. Is that the *People's* Educational Center?

MR. WOOD. Yes. Eddie Dmytryk—I referred to him—is the instructor there.

Edward Dmytryk first appeared before the Committee on October 29, 1947.

MR. DMYTRYK. I was born on September 4, 1908, in Grand Forks, British Columbia, Canada.

INVESTIGATOR. When and how did you become a citizen of the United States, Mr. Dmytryk?

MR. DMYTRYK. I was naturalized in '39 in Los Angeles.

Edward Dmytryk (*UPI*).

INVESTIGATOR. How long have you been a motion picture director?

MR. DMYTRYK. Since '39.

INVESTIGATOR. With what studios are you associated?

MR. DMYTRYK. RKO.

INVESTIGATOR. What studios were you associated with in the past?

MR. DMYTRYK. Most of my years were spent at Paramount.

INVESTIGATOR. Would you give the Committee the names of some of the pictures you have directed?

MR. DMYTRYK. Mr. Chairman, I have a statement here that I'd like to make.

THE CHAIRMAN. Let me see the statement. *After looking at the statement.* It is not pertinent to this inquiry. The Chair rules it cannot be read.

MR. DMYTRYK. Mr. Chairman, since this statement concerns questions as to the effect of this investigation—

THE CHAIRMAN. The Chair has ruled that the statement was not pertinent. The Chief Investigator will ask questions, and you will please answer them.

INVESTIGATOR. Mr. Dmytryk, are you a member of the Screen Directors Guild?

MR. DMYTRYK. Mr. Stripling, I feel these questions are designed to—

THE CHAIRMAN. Just a minute. It is not up to you to "feel" what the design is. It is up to you to be responsive to the questions.

MR. DMYTRYK. Most other witnesses were given the right to answer as they pleased. Some went on at length—

INVESTIGATOR. Pardon me, Mr. Dmytryk. About how long a time would you require to answer whether you were a member of the Screen Directors Guild? Would five minutes be long enough?

MR. DMYTRYK. It would take me a lot less than five minutes.

THE CHAIRMAN. It would take you five minutes to answer whether you are a member of the Screen Directors Guild?

MR. DMYTRYK. I said a lot *less* than five minutes, Mr. Chairman.

THE CHAIRMAN. Can't you answer yes or no, are you a member of the Screen Directors Guild?

MR. DMYTRYK. There aren't many questions that can be answered yes or no—

THE CHAIRMAN. I am referring to this this one question.

MR. DMYTRYK. I would like to answer it in my own way.

THE CHAIRMAN. That question *can* be answered yes or no!

MR. DMYTRYK. I don't think I'll take long enough to bore you, Mr. Chairman.

THE CHAIRMAN. Go ahead.

MR. DMYTRYK. This kind of questioning is designed to bring about a split in the guilds at a time when we've just succeeded in getting unity between them. I was an officer of the Screen Directors Guild—

INVESTIGATOR. Are you now, or have you ever been, a member of the Communist Party?

MR. DMYTRYK. Well, Mr. Stripling, there is a question of constitutional rights here.

THE CHAIRMAN. When did you learn about the Constitution? Tell me when you learned about the Constitution!

MR. DMYTRYK. I *first* learned about the Constitution in high school.

CM 1. Let's have the answer to the other question.

MR. DMYTRYK. I was asked when I learned about the Constitution.

INVESTIGATOR. The first question, Mr. Dmytryk, was: Are you now, or have you ever been, a member of the Communist Party?

MR. DMYTRYK. All right, gentlemen, if you will keep your questions simple, and one at a time, I'll be glad to answer.

INVESTIGATOR. That is *very* simple.

MR. DMYTRYK. The Chairman asked me another question.

THE CHAIRMAN. I withdraw the other question.

MR. DMYTRYK. The Constitution does not ask that such a question be answered in the way that Mr. Stripling wants it answered. What organizations I belong to, what I think, and what I say cannot be questioned by this Committee.

INVESTIGATOR. Then you refuse to answer the question?

MR. DMYTRYK. I do not refuse to answer it. I answered it—in my own way.

INVESTIGATOR. You haven't answered whether or not you are a member of the Communist Party.

MR. DMYTRYK. I answered by saying I do not think you have the right to ask—

INVESTIGATOR. Mr. Chairman, it is apparent that the witness is pursuing the same line as—

THE CHAIRMAN. The witness is excused.

Ring Lardner, Jr. came before the Committee the following day.

INVESTIGATOR. When and where were you born, Mr. Lardner?

MR. LARDNER. August 19, 1915, in Chicago, Illinois.

INVESTIGATOR. What is your occupation?

MR. LARDNER. A writer.

INVESTIGATOR. How long have you been a writer?

MR. LARDNER. I have been a writer about ten years. Mr. Chairman, I have a short statement I would like to make. *The witness hands statement to The Chairman. The witness hands statement to the Investigator.*

THE CHAIRMAN. Mr. Lardner, the Committee is unanimous that, after you testify, you may read your statement.

MR. LARDNER. Thank you.

INVESTIGATOR. Mr. Lardner, are you a member of the Screen Writers Guild?

MR. LARDNER. Mr. Stripling, I want to be cooperative about this but there are limits to my cooperation. I don't want to help you smash this particular guild, or to infiltrate the motion-picture business in any way, to control what the American people can see and hear in their motion-picture theaters.

THE CHAIRMAN. Now, Mr. Lardner, don't do like the others, if I were you, or you will never read your statement. I would suggest—

MR. LARDNER. Mr. Chairman, let me—

THE CHAIRMAN. —you be responsive to the question.

MR. LARDNER. I am—

THE CHAIRMAN. The question is: Are you a member of the Screen Writers Guild?

MR. LARDNER. I understood I *would* be permitted to read the statement, Mr. Chairman.

Ring Lardner, Jr. (*Acme Photo*).

THE CHAIRMAN. Yes, after you've finished with the questions and answers.

MR. LARDNER. Yes.

THE CHAIRMAN. But you haven't answered the questions.

MR. LARDNER. Well, I am going to answer the questions, but I don't think you qualified your statement that I'd be allowed to read this statement.

THE CHAIRMAN. I will qualify it now. If you refuse to answer the question, you will not read your statement.

MR. LARDNER. That is an indirect way of saying you don't want me to read the statement.

THE CHAIRMAN. You know right now you are not going to answer the question?

MR. LARDNER. No, I am going to answer the question.

THE CHAIRMAN. All right, then, answer that question.

MR. LARDNER. All right, sir. I think I have to consider why the question is asked—

THE CHAIRMAN. *We* will determine why the question was asked! We want to know whether you are a member of the Screen Writers Guild.

MR. LARDNER. Yes—

THE CHAIRMAN. That is a very simple question. You can answer that yes or no. You don't have to go into a long harangue. If you want to make a speech, you know where you can go out there.

MR. LARDNER. Well, I am not very good in haranguing, and I won't try it, but, if you can make me answer this question, tomorrow, it seems to me, you could ask somebody whether he believed in spiritualism.

THE CHAIRMAN. There is no chance of our asking anyone whether they believe in spiritualism, and you know it. That is just plain silly!

MR. LARDNER. You might—

THE CHAIRMAN. Now, you haven't learned your lines very well.

MR. LARDNER. Well—

THE CHAIRMAN. I want to know whether you can answer the question yes or no.

MR. LARDNER. If you asked somebody that, you might ask him—

THE CHAIRMAN. Well, now, never mind what we *might* ask him. We are asking you now, Are you a member of the Screen Writers Guild?

MR. LARDNER. But—

THE CHAIRMAN. You are an American—

MR. LARDNER. But that is a question—

THE CHAIRMAN. —and Americans should not be afraid to answer that.

MR. LARDNER. I am also concerned, as an American, with the question of whether this Committee has the right to ask me—

THE CHAIRMAN. Well, we *have* got the right, and until you prove we *haven't* got the right, you have to answer that question.

MR. LARDNER. As I said, if you ask somebody, say, about spiritualism—

THE CHAIRMAN. You're a witness, aren't you? Aren't you a witness?

MR. LARDNER. Mr. Chairman—

THE CHAIRMAN. Aren't you a witness here?

MR. LARDNER. Yes, I am.

THE CHAIRMAN. All right, then, a Congressional Committee is asking you: Are you a member of the Screen Writers Guild? Answer it yes or no.

MR. LARDNER. Well, to answer that—

THE CHAIRMAN. All right, put the next question. Go to the sixty-four-dollar question.

THE WITNESS. I haven't—

THE CHAIRMAN. Go to the next question.

INVESTIGATOR. Mr. Lardner, are you now, or have you ever been, a member of the Communist Party?

MR. LARDNER. Well, I would like to answer that question, too.

INVESTIGATOR. Mr. Lardner, the charge has been made that the Screen Writers Guild which you are a member of, whether you admit it or not, has in it members of the Communist Party. This Committee is seeking to determine the extent of Communist infiltration in the Screen Writers Guild.

MR. LARDNER. Yes.

INVESTIGATOR. Now, are you, or have you ever been, a member of the Communist Party?

MR. LARDNER. It seems to me you are trying to discredit the Screen Writers Guild through me, and the motion-picture industry through the Screen Writers Guild, and our whole practice of freedom of expression.

INVESTIGATOR. If you and others are members of the Communist Party, you are the ones who are discrediting the Screen Writers Guild.

MR. LARDNER. I am trying to answer the question by stating, first, what I feel about the purpose of the question which, as I say, is to discredit the whole motion-picture industry.

THE CHAIRMAN. You won't say anything "first." You are refusing to answer this question.

MR. LARDNER. My understanding is, as an American resident—

THE CHAIRMAN. Never mind your understanding! There is a question: Are you, or have you ever been, a member of the Communist Party?

MR. LARDNER. I could answer exactly the way you want, Mr. Chairman—

THE CHAIRMAN. No—

Robert E. Stripling (*Acme Photo*).

MR. LARDNER. —but I think that is a—

THE CHAIRMAN. It is not a question of our wanting you to answer that. It is a very simple question. Any real American would be proud to answer the question, "Are you, or have you ever been, a member of the Communist Party?"—any *real* American.

MR. LARDNER. It depends on the circumstances. I could answer it, but if I did, I would hate myself in the morning.

THE CHAIRMAN. Leave the witness chair!

MR. LARDNER. It was a question that would—

THE CHAIRMAN. Leave the witness chair!

MR. LARDNER. Because it is a question—

THE CHAIRMAN, *pounding gavel*. Leave the witness chair!

MR. LARDNER. I think I am leaving by force!

THE CHAIRMAN. Sergeant, take the witness away! *A Sergeant takes him away.*

THE CHAIRMAN. Mr. Stripling, next witness.

INVESTIGATOR. Mr. Russell, you were detailed to determine whether or not Ring Lardner, Jr., was ever a member of the Communist Party?

2ND INVESTIGATOR. I was.

INVESTIGATOR. Will you give the Committee the benefit of your investigation?

2ND INVESTIGATOR. This Communist Party registration card bears the number 47180. It is made out in the name of Ring L., which, during the course of the investigation, developed to be the name of Ring Lardner, Jr.

So Dmytryk and Lardner and their eight colleagues went to jail, and so, as it happened, did the Chairman of the Committee, J. Parnell Thomas, who had been stealing the taxpayers' money. Before the grand jury Thomas invoked the Fifth Amendment. Eventually he would receive a presidential pardon from Truman, but before this happened he and Ring Lardner, Jr. met again. In Lardner's words:

The blue prison fatigues hung loosely on the weary, perspiring man whose path across the quadrangle was about to meet mine. I felt I looked comparatively dapper in the same costume after a day of mild stenographic labor in the Office of Classification and Parole, but his job kept him in the August sun all day. He was custodian of the chicken yard at the Federal Correctional Institution, Danbury, Connecticut, and his name was J. Parnell Thomas. He had lost a good deal of weight, and his face, round and scarlet at our last encounter, was deeply lined and sallow. I recognized him, however, and he recognized me, but we did not speak. It would have been hard for either of us to pick up the thread.

The first person in show business to testify to former
Party membership was Larry Parks, star of two then
recent movies, *The Jolson Story* and *Jolson Sings Again*.
Parks spent a whole day with the Committee, March 21,
1951.

MORNING

INVESTIGATOR. The Committee on Un-American Activities
has succeeded in exposing Communists' infiltration
into labor organizations, with the result that the organizations have rid themselves of Communist domination,
and that the Congress has been informed of important
facts as the basis for legislative action. The testimony
of Matthew Cvetic virtually destroyed the power of the
Communist Party in western Pennsylvania. Then there
have been many witnesses who have told how they
were duped into joining the Party, the activities they
observed as members, and their reasons for breaking.
They have performed a service of inestimable value to
their country and should receive the plaudits of their
fellow citizens. The hearing today is the first of a series
designed to accomplish the same results in the entertainment field. It is hoped that any witness who made the
mistake of associating himself with the Communist
Party will have sufficient courage and loyalty to make
an honest disclosure of all he knows. I would like to
call, as the first witness, Mr. Larry Parks. Are you rep-
resented by counsel, Mr. Parks?

MR. PARKS. Yes, I am.

INVESTIGATOR. Will counsel identify himself?

MR. MANDEL. Louis Mandel, 1501 Broadway, New York
City. Mr. Parks has prepared a statement. It will be

Larry Parks and Adrian Scott, just before Parks took the
stand (*Acme Photo*).

enlightening to the Committee as his testimony unfolds. May he read that statement?

THE CHAIRMAN. At the conclusion of his testimony.

MR. MANDEL. In fairness to the witness, I would urge that he be permitted to read the statement now. There is a connecting link to what he will testify.

THE CHAIRMAN. Proceed, Mr. Tavenner.

INVESTIGATOR. Mr. Parks, when and where were you born?

MR. PARKS. I was born on a farm in Kansas. The closest town would be Olathe.

INVESTIGATOR. Will you relate the details regarding your educational background?

MR. PARKS. I moved when quite small to Illinois, attended the high school in Joliet, graduated from the University of Illinois, where I majored in chemistry and minored in physics. I sometimes wonder how I got in my present line of work!

INVESTIGATOR. Mr. Parks, there has been testimony regarding a number of organizations in Hollywood, such as the Actors' Laboratory Theater. Have you been connected with any of those?

MR. PARKS. I have.

INVESTIGATOR. Will you state their names? I will hand you the list.

MR. PARKS, *looking at sheet of paper.* Well, I'm familiar with the Actors' Laboratory.

INVESTIGATOR. Did you hold any position in that organization?

MR. PARKS. For a time I was sort of honorary treasurer. *He reads the list in silence.*

INVESTIGATOR. Proceed.

MR. PARKS. I was a member of the Hollywood Independent Citizens Committee of the Arts, Sciences, and Professions.

19

THE CHAIRMAN. We will have to ask the photographers not to block the view.

INVESTIGATOR. Now, referring back to the Actors' Laboratory, of which you were treasurer?

MR. PARKS. In name, yes.

INVESTIGATOR. "In name"?

MR. PARKS. My job was to sign a batch of checks, and that's the extent of my knowledge of the money matters.

INVESTIGATOR. Will you tell the Committee whether or not there were Communists in these various organizations?

MR. PARKS. I can say yes to that.

INVESTIGATOR. Well, who were these Communists?

MR. PARKS. I don't know. There were Communists attached to the Lab. But this was not a Communist organization in any sense of the word!

INVESTIGATOR. Well, were there Communists attached to these other organizations you say you were a member of?

MR. PARKS. I don't know.

INVESTIGATOR. But do you recall that, at the Actors' Laboratory, there were members of the Communist Party?

MR. PARKS. That's true.

INVESTIGATOR. Did those Party members endeavor to obtain control?

MR. PARKS. No, the Lab was a school for acting and sort of a showcase for actors.

INVESTIGATOR. Well, what was your opportunity to observe that there were Communists in that organization?

MR. PARKS. I knew them as Communists.

INVESTIGATOR. Well, what had been your opportunity to know them as Communists?

Pause.

MR. PARKS. In my opinion, there is a great difference between being a Communist in '41 and being a Communist in '51. *Pause.* I was a member of the Communist Party in '41.

INVESTIGATOR. Tell the Committee the circumstances under which you became a member of the Communist Party; and, if you left the Party, when you did and why.

MR. PARKS. Being a member of the Party fulfilled certain needs of a young man who was liberal in thought, idealistic, who was for the underprivileged, the underdog. I felt it fulfilled these needs. Being a Communist in '51, in *this* situation, is a different kettle of fish. A great power is trying to take over the world. This is the difference!

INVESTIGATOR. You didn't realize that the purpose of the Communist Party was to take over other segments of the world in '41? But you do realize that in '51?

MR. PARKS. This is in no way an apology for anything I've done, you see, because I feel I have done nothing wrong, ever. In '41 the purposes, as I knew them, simply fulfilled—at least I thought they would fulfill—a certain idealism, a certain feeling of being for the underdog, which I am today, this minute. This didn't work out. . . . I wasn't particularly interested after I did become a member—I attended very few meetings and petered out the same way I drifted in. I petered out in '44 or '45.

INVESTIGATOR. Your Communist registration card for the year 1944 bore the number 46954 and for the year 1945 the number 47344. Does that refresh your recollection?

MR. PARKS. No, sir, it doesn't. Because I never had a Party card.

Pause.

INVESTIGATOR. Now, do I infer that by '46 you had broken with the Party?

MR. PARKS. Correct.

INVESTIGATOR. Will you state to the Committee where you first became a member of the Party?

MR. PARKS. Hollywood, California.

INVESTIGATOR. Who recruited you into the Party?

MR. PARKS. A man by the name of Davidson, I believe.

INVESTIGATOR. What was Davidson's first name and position?

MR. PARKS. I don't remember his first name. I haven't seen him for ten years. And I don't know what his position was.

INVESTIGATOR. Where did he live?

MR. PARKS. I have no idea.

INVESTIGATOR. What was his occupation?

MR. PARKS. I don't know either.

INVESTIGATOR. Can you give us some descriptive data on the individual?

MR. PARKS. Average-looking, young, dark hair.
Pause.

INVESTIGATOR. Well, what were the circumstances under which you met?

MR. PARKS. This is hard for me to recall, too.

INVESTIGATOR. Was it at a meeting in your home or where?

MR. PARKS. I *really* don't remember. I'm being as honest as I know how!

INVESTIGATOR. I just wanted you to give the Committee what information you recall about how you got into the Communist Party.

MR. PARKS. I was a good deal younger then—about twenty-five—with certain liberal tendencies, idealism.

INVESTIGATOR. Did you seek this individual out, or did he seek you out?

MR. PARKS. I certainly didn't seek *him* out. It's hard for me to say whether he sought *me* out.

INVESTIGATOR. Did others counsel you in regard to your uniting with the Communist Party—before you were recruited by this Davidson?

MR. PARKS. No, I did it of my own volition.

INVESTIGATOR. Were you assigned to a Party cell?

MR. PARKS. I was.

INVESTIGATOR. What was the name of that cell, and where was it located?

MR. PARKS. Well, it had no name that I know of.

INVESTIGATOR. Well now, you were a member of that group from '41 to '45?

MR. PARKS. That's correct.

INVESTIGATOR. Will you tell us what you know about the organization of the Communist Party during that time?

MR. PARKS. Well, I was a pretty bad member by their lights. Didn't attend too many meetings—maybe ten, twelve, fifteen. What I know about the Communist Party is very little.

INVESTIGATOR. Do you know whether the writers and actors in Hollywood were members of any particular branch or group of the Communist Party?

MR. PARKS. I know that certain actors were a group that met. The other things I do not know.

INVESTIGATOR. Well, were there several groups to which the actors belonged, depending upon the geographical location of the actor?

MR. PARKS. I wouldn't say for certain. I'm not under that impression.

INVESTIGATOR. Well, who was the chairman of the group?

MR. PARKS. It had no chairman that I know of.

INVESTIGATOR. Well, who was the secretary?

MR. PARKS. I don't recall. I don't know if there were any actual officers.

INVESTIGATOR. Well, to whom did you pay your dues?

MR. PARKS. This is hard for me to answer, too, because the few times I paid dues were to different people.

INVESTIGATOR. Well, was Communist Party literature distributed to the members?

MR. PARKS. Certain pamphlets were available if you wished to buy them.

INVESTIGATOR. Who had charge of the distribution or sale?

MR. PARKS. Well, this I don't know either. The pamphlets were there. You could buy them if you wished.

INVESTIGATOR. Well, was there any secret about who was handling the literature of the Party?

MR. PARKS. No.

Pause.

INVESTIGATOR. What was the total membership of this cell?

MR. PARKS. I would say it went up to maybe, oh, possibly ten or twelve.

INVESTIGATOR. Did the personnel change between '41 and '45?

MR. PARKS. I attended rather irregularly, and at some of the meetings I would see someone I didn't recognize, and I would never see them again.

INVESTIGATOR. Did Party organizers appear before your group from time to time—people from the East, let us say?

MR. PARKS. No, I don't recall ever seeing any big shot.

INVESTIGATOR. You are acquainted with V. J. Jerome?

MR. PARKS. I don't believe I've ever seen him.

INVESTIGATOR. Are you acquainted with Lionel Stander?

MR. PARKS. I've met him.

INVESTIGATOR. Have you ever attended a Communist Party meeting with him?

MR. PARKS. I don't recall ever attending a Communist Party meeting with Lionel Stander.

INVESTIGATOR. Do you know whether he's a Party member?

MR. PARKS. No.

INVESTIGATOR. Are you acquainted with Karen Morley?

MR. PARKS. I am.

INVESTIGATOR. Is she a member of the Communist Party?

Pause.

MR. PARKS. Well, counsel, these—I would prefer not to mention names. I don't think it's fair to people. I've come to you at your request. I'll tell you everything I know about myself, because I feel I've done nothing wrong, and I'll answer any question you'd like to put to me about myself. I would prefer not to mention other people's names.

CM 1. Do you take the same position with respect to the leaders of the Communist movement?

MR. PARKS. I do, because I don't know the leaders of the Communist movement.

CM 1. You know who was active in the movement in California?

MR. PARKS. I only know the names of people who attended certain meetings. These were not leaders of the Communist Party.

CM 1. Who directed the meetings you attended?

MR. PARKS. The meetings consisted mainly of—we were in a war then—discussions of how the war was going, current events, problems of actors in their work. Does that answer your question, Congressman?

CM 1. It's an answer.

MR. PARKS. Hmm?

CM 1. It's an answer.

MR. PARKS. I'd like to answer your question. . . .

CM 1. Who directed the activities this group were engaged in?

MR. PARKS. No one to my knowledge *directed* activities.

CM 2. Who would call the meetings together?

Karen Morley and her attorney, Vito Marcantonio (*UPI*).

MR. PARKS. Well, I don't really know.

CM 2. Did you have a set, scheduled meeting once every week, or was it upon the call of some individual?

MR. PARKS. Various individuals would call. I don't believe there was any set—

CM 2. Certainly it wasn't run by mental telepathy!

MR. PARKS. No. I didn't say that. I say certain individuals would call, and, to the best of my knowledge, there was no set schedule.

CM 2. Somebody had to issue a call?

MR. PARKS. That's correct.

CM 2. Did *you* ever issue a call?

MR. PARKS. No.

CM 2. Then, somebody would have to tell you when and where the meetings would take place, is that not true?

MR. PARKS. I would get a call from a member of the group and they would say, "Let's have a meeting tonight, tomorrow night."

CM 3. Were the meetings always held at the same place?

MR. PARKS. No.

CM 3. Were they held in halls or in your own homes?

MR. PARKS. These were held at homes.

CM 3. Did you ever have meetings at *your* home?

MR. PARKS. Never.

CM 3. Where were some of the meetings held?

Pause.

MR. PARKS. These were people like myself, small-type people, no different than myself in any respect at all, no different than you or I.

CM 3. Where were some of the meetings held?

MR. PARKS. As I say, in various homes in Hollywood.

CM 3. Can you name some?

Pause.

MR. PARKS. Well, if you will allow this, I would prefer not

to mention names. These were people—like myself—who have done nothing wrong, ever. I mean, along this line. I'm sure none of us is perfect. Again, the question of judgment certainly is there, but these are people—

THE CHAIRMAN. Just a moment. Do you entertain the feeling that these parties you were associated with are likewise guiltless of any wrong?

MR. PARKS. This is my opinion: that these are people who did nothing wrong, people like myself.

THE CHAIRMAN. Mr. Parks, in what way would it be injurious to them to divulge their identities when at no time did they do wrong?

Pause.

MR. PARKS. If you think it's easy—I've worked hard in my profession, climbed up the ladder a bit—if you think it's easy for me to appear before this Committee and testify, you're mistaken. This is a very difficult job for me. One of the reasons is that, as an actor, my activity depends a great deal on the public. To be called before this Committee at your request has a certain inference, a certain innuendo that you're not loyal to this country. This is not true. I am speaking for myself. This is not true. But the inference, the innuendo is there as far as the public is concerned. Also, as a representative of a great industry—as an actor who is fairly well known, in that respect I am a representative. . . . This is a great industry! At this time it is being investigated for Communist influence—

THE CHAIRMAN. Don't you think the public is entitled to know about it?

MR. PARKS. Hmm?

THE CHAIRMAN. Don't you feel the public is entitled to know about it?

28

MR. PARKS. I certainly do, and I'm opening myself wide to any question that you can ask me. I'll answer as honestly as I know how. And at this time, as I say, the industry is—it's like taking a pot shot at a wounded animal, because the industry is not in as good a shape as it has been—economically, it's been pretty tough. This is a great industry! And I don't say this only because it has been kind to *me*. It has a very important job to do, to entertain people, in certain respects to call attention to certain evils, but mainly to entertain, and I feel they've done a great job. When our country has needed help, the industry has been in the forefront of that help!

INVESTIGATOR. You are basing your reluctance to testify on the great job that the moving-picture industry is doing? *Pause.*

MR. PARKS. On naming names, it is my opinion that the few people I could name, these names would not be of service to the Committee: I am sure you know who they are. These people are like myself, and I have done nothing wrong. I also feel that this is not—to be asked to name names like this is not—in the way of American justice as we know it. We as Americans have all been brought up to believe it's a bad thing to force a man to do this. I've been brought up that way, I'm sure you have. . . . This is not the American way!

THE CHAIRMAN. Well, I'm glad to give considerable leeway to the range of your statement, because I'm curious to understand what your reasons are for declining to answer the question.

MR. PARKS. I'm not declining. I'm asking you if you would not press me on this.

THE CHAIRMAN. I'm not going to press the point unless other members of the Committee wish to.

29

CM 2. Are any of the members of your cell still active in the Communist Party?

MR. PARKS. I can't say this, Congressman. I divorced myself completely. I know what I *think:* that ninety-nine percent of them are not.

CM 2. If you knew people in Hollywood that were identified with the Party *then,* would you be reluctant to cite their names if they were active members *at the present time?*

MR. PARKS. I would be reluctant on only one score: that I don't think it's good for an American to be forced to do this. But I feel that the people I knew are *not* members of the Communist Party at the present time. If they are, they shouldn't be!

CM 2. If you had knowledge of a man who committed murder, you wouldn't be hesitant to give that information to the proper authorities?

MR. PARKS. That is correct.

CM 2. I assume you share our belief that an active member of the Communist Party believes in overthrowing our Government by force and violence. Now, if you would give information concerning a man you know has committed murder, wouldn't you give information of a man you knew to be working to overthrow our Government by force and violence?

MR. PARKS. If I knew a man who committed murder, which is against the law of our land, I would name him immediately. The other thing—well, even now it is *not* against the law of our land. *Pause.* You understand the difference I mean?

CM 2. So when we are drafting men to fight Communist aggression, you feel it is not your duty as an American citizen to give the Committee the benefit of what knowledge you might have?

MR. PARKS. I think there is a difference, Congressman, between people who would harm our country and people like myself, who, as I feel, did nothing wrong—

CM 2. I'm not questioning the point when you say people like you may be misguided or were members of the Party because of faulty judgment, but you don't believe that anyone can be naive enough to be an active member of the Communist Party *today* and not know what he's doing?

MR. PARKS. That's correct.

CM 2. For that reason I can't see your consistency in saying you won't name someone you know, today, who is an active member of the Party.

MR. PARKS. But I don't know *anyone* today who is an active member of the Party.

CM 2. If you did know, you would tell?

Pause.

MR. PARKS. Yes, I think I would.

Pause.

INVESTIGATOR. Mr. Parks, your argument is that this Committee should investigate Communism but should not find out who is a Communist.

MR. PARKS. No, this is not my argument at all!

INVESTIGATOR. You are taking the position that it is not important to find out who may be in Communism in Hollywood—

MR. PARKS. No.

INVESTIGATOR. —rather than for this Committee to determine what its obligations are under the statute which created it to investigate Communism?

MR. PARKS. No, counsel, I didn't say *this*!

INVESTIGATOR. But isn't it the result of your argument?

MR. PARKS. No, counsel, what I say is that the few people I knew are as loyal to this country as you.

31

INVESTIGATOR. And if every witness were permitted to take that position the extent of the investigation would be *limited* by the attitude of the witness, wouldn't it?

MR. PARKS. But I told you the circumstances surrounding my small activity with the Communist Party, and this makes a difference.

INVESTIGATOR. In your judgment?

MR. PARKS. Not only in my judgment. I know these people were like me, and the most you can accuse them of is a lack of judgment. I say none of this in apology for what I did, because a young man at twenty-five, if he's not a liberal, if he's not full of idealism, is not worth his salt. If you make a mistake in judgment like this, I don't believe it is serious!

INVESTIGATOR. Yes, but if every witness would be the final judge of when a thing was serious and when it was not, how could the Committee carry out its statutory duty?

MR. PARKS. I'm asking that—

INVESTIGATOR. And I'm asking that you see the other side.

MR. PARKS. I do see the other side.

INVESTIGATOR. Now, Mr. Parks, you have placed Hollywood on a very high pedestal.

MR. PARKS. I have.

INVESTIGATOR. But there has been testimony involving the scientific professions, persons in government, persons in numerous industries, and I take it no preference should be allowed to *your* profession over any other calling?

MR. PARKS. That is true. I was probably the poorest member of the Communist Party that has existed, and the few people I knew, you probably know their names! I can see no way this would be of help to the Committee. If it were really consequential, I would do it. But you must realize—

INVESTIGATOR. Pardon me?

MR. PARKS. You must realize that, inconsequential as I was, the few people I knew . . . it's *distasteful* to me to be forced into this position!

INVESTIGATOR. It is a distasteful position to be in.

MR. PARKS. And I—

INVESTIGATOR. You understand the purposes of this organization. If you would be equally frank with regard to other people who are connected with this organization, the Committee would be permitted to function. And, therefore, I am going to ask you who acted as secretary of this group.

MR. PARKS. And I can honestly say I do not know.

Pause.

INVESTIGATOR. Do you know Elizabeth Leech?

MR. PARKS. I don't recall an Elizabeth Leech.

INVESTIGATOR. Do you know a person by the name of Elizabeth Glenn?

MR. PARKS. To the best of my knowledge, I do not.

INVESTIGATOR. Do you know a person by the name of Marjorie Potts?

MR. PARKS. I do not. I don't recall ever meeting these people!

INVESTIGATOR. Now, do you know Karen Morley?

Pause.

MR. PARKS. I do.

INVESTIGATOR. Was Karen Morley a member of this group with you?

MR. PARKS. And I ask you again, counsel, to reconsider forcing me to name names. I told you I was a member only for a short time, and I don't think this is American justice, to force me to do this, when I have come three thousand miles and—

CM 1. Mr. Chairman, may I ask counsel a question? *To the*

33

Investigator: How can it be material to this inquiry to have the names of people, when we already know them? By insisting that this man testify as to names, aren't we overlooking the fact that we want to know what the *organization* did, how it attempted to influence the thinking of the American people through the arts?

MR. PARKS. May I answer your question?

CM 1. No.

INVESTIGATOR. Some of these individuals have evaded service of process, so we cannot bring them here. That is one point. Another is that this Committee ought to receive *proof* of information which it has in its files. There would be no way to investigate Communist infiltration into labor without asking who *are* Communists in labor.

CM 1. But isn't it more important to learn the extent of the activity, and the purpose of the organization, than to get a list of names of bleeding hearts and fools and suckers?

INVESTIGATOR. As to organizations, that *was* the subject of much testimony.

CM 1. May I ask the witness a question, Mr. Chairman?

THE CHAIRMAN. Yes, Mr. Walter.

CM 1. Were you instructed to influence the thinking of the American people through stage or screen?

MR. PARKS. I was never instructed to do this, and I think it is evident that this was not done.

CM 1. Was it talked about? Was it the purpose of the Communist organization to set up a hard core in Hollywood that would slant pictures and performances?

MR. PARKS. First of all, it's impossible to do this as an actor. I was never asked to.

THE CHAIRMAN. Wouldn't the *writer* be in a position to very decidedly slant—

MR. PARKS. A script passes through too many hands. It is my opinion that this is an impossibility.

THE CHAIRMAN. And didn't happen?

MR. PARKS. I don't believe that this ever happened.

THE CHAIRMAN. Now, you're leaving an impression there was nothing off-color about the people in your group. How then could it reflect against the members of this group for the names to be known—any more than if they belonged to the YMCA?

MR. PARKS. I feel as I do because myself I am a good example. As I said, it's not easy for me to be here. Anybody who thinks it is is out of their mind. It is doubtful whether, after appearing before this Committee, my career will continue, it is *extremely* doubtful. . . . For coming here and telling you the truth! There were other things open to me, but, feeling that I have not done anything wrong, I will tell you the truth.

CM 4. Mr. Parks, have you any knowledge of the efforts of the movie industry to clean out subversive influence?

MR. PARKS. This is common knowledge.

CM 4. Is it *your* knowledge?

MR. PARKS. When I say "common knowledge" I mean mine, yours, everybody's.
  Pause.

CM 4. A few minutes ago, you said you were honorary treasurer. Your duty was to sign a batch of checks.

MR. PARKS. That's right.

CM 4. To whom were those checks written?

MR. PARKS. Well, these were to pay the office help, the secretaries, the clean-up man, the teachers, electric company. . . .

CM 4. How many secretaries and what office help for what organizations?

MR. PARKS. For the Actors' Lab.

CM 4. How many secretaries?

MR. PARKS. It varied. From none to three or four.

CM 4. Was this one cell limited to members of the actors' profession?

MR. PARKS. I believe it was.

CM 4. And you had a social affair? Did you have refreshments?

MR. PARKS. Yes. Coffee.

Laughter.

I'm serious when I say that! Coffee! Doughnuts!

CM 4. Did the cell have dues?

MR. PARKS. It did.

CM 4. How much were the dues?

MR. PARKS. Well, I couldn't have contributed more than fifty, sixty dollars.

CM 4. You were connected with this cell from '41 to '45, yet you only paid a total of fifty or sixty dollars?

MR. PARKS. Well, the dues, as I recall, when you weren't working, were about seventy-five cents a month, and if you were working I think you paid some percentage. I didn't.

CM 4. You were idealistic, liberal, progressive at the age of twenty-five, and that is perhaps one reason you joined the Communist Party—

MR. PARKS. No, that is *the* reason.

CM 4. Didn't that cell make efforts to increase its own membership in Hollywood?

MR. PARKS. I personally never made such an effort.

CM 4. No, but you heard reports of what was being done by the cell?

MR. PARKS. That's correct.

CM 4. Well, what reports were given?

MR. PARKS. I don't remember. It's been a long time.

CM 4. Well, now, you notice, Parks, at this time I'm deliberately avoiding asking you names!

MR. PARKS. Yes.

CM 4. I am assuming you want to be helpful to the Committee and tell the activities of the cell!

MR. PARKS. That's correct, and I'm doing this.

CM 4. Now, manifestly, the cell was trying to increase its membership, wasn't it?

MR. PARKS. That's correct.

CM 4. You testified that you heard reports—

MR. PARKS. Well, as I say—

CM 4. —of what the cell was doing to increase its membership.

MR. PARKS. Well, you're really going a bit further than I said, Congressman.

CM 4. Well, you go as far as you honestly can and tell us what activities the cell participated in to increase its membership.

MR. PARKS. Well, I think certain members of the group approached people about becoming a member of the Communist Party. I myself never did this.

CM 4. Well, names of prospective members were read off in· your presence, or possibilities were read off, weren't they?

MR. PARKS. It's possible that this was done.

CM 4. Well, *was* it done?

MR. PARKS. As I say, it's been a long time.

Pause.

CM 4. Was any difference in philosophy between Communism and our form of government ever discussed in the cell?

Silence.

What *did* you discuss, besides drinking coffee?

MR. PARKS. We didn't discuss drinking coffee! The war was going on, and this was the major topic of conversation. The discussions also had to do with actors—how we could get more money, better conditions.

CM 4. Well, was it discussed among you that you could get

more money as a member of the Communist Party than as a plain Democrat or Republican?

MR. PARKS. No, this was never discussed.

CM 4. Why did you join? What was membership in this cell going to do for you in Hollywood?

MR. PARKS. As a man of twenty-five, with ideals and a feeling for the underdog, I felt this was a legitimate party. Like the Democrats or Republicans. I felt this was the most *liberal* of the parties. . . . I was a registered Democrat. I still am. From that time and before, I've voted the straight Democratic ticket! This was the practical thing to do. The other was an idealistic thing. . . .

CM 4. How many years were you in that cell before you began to be disillusioned?

MR. PARKS. Well, "disillusion" is not the word I would choose.

THE CHAIRMAN. Do I understand, sir, that you are *not yet* disillusioned?

MR. PARKS. No, no. Don't bend it! It was a question of lack of interest, of not finding the things that I thought I would find.

CM 4. Did it come clearly to you that the Communist Party was part of an international conspiracy against our form of government?

MR. PARKS. No.

CM 4. Did you come to the conclusion that the Communist Party program was aimed at world domination?

MR. PARKS. Not at that time.

CM 4. When did you come to that conclusion, if at all?

MR. PARKS. Well, the way most everybody has: with recent events in the history of our country and the world.

CM 3. Were there members of the Communist Party who spoke to your group?

MR. PARKS. There was one instance.

CM 3. Can you give his name?

Pause.

MR. PARKS. Again I wish you would not press me.

CM 5. Mr. Parks, do you now know that, at the time you belonged to the Communist Party, it was a subversive organization?

MR. PARKS. A great change has occurred.

CM 1. You feel that the "do-gooders" have gotten out of it and there is nothing remaining except the hard-boiled politicians?

MR. PARKS. I agree.

CM 5. Mr. Parks, how could you know how *other* members of your cell felt about the Party?

MR. PARKS. Well, during the war a common purpose united all the people of this country. . . .

CM 5. I don't think you're answering my question, Mr. Parks. I realize your reluctance in telling the membership of your organization.

MR. PARKS. Would you repeat the question then?

CM 5. We had a witness down here last year, Lee Pressman, who was likewise reluctant to answer questions concerning his association with a Communist Party cell, but eventually he did, and it did the Committee good. I *understand* your reluctance, but the Committee is legally organized and has a function.

MR. PARKS. I agree.

CM 5. As such it has the right to inquire as to the names of members of the Communist Party.

MR. PARKS. That is your right.

INVESTIGATOR. Mr. Parks, you are no doubt acquainted with Samuel G. Wood, producer and director?

Parks nods.

Sam G. Wood testified as follows: "The Laboratory

Theater is under the control of the Communist Party. Any kid that goes in there with American ideals hasn't a chance in the world." Do you agree?

MR. PARKS. I disagree.

INVESTIGATOR. You agree that Mr. Wood is a man of honor?

MR. PARKS. But I disagree with *this*.

INVESTIGATOR. But, in light of that testimony, do you still feel *you* should be the judge as to whether or not you should testify—

MR. PARKS. At no time did I say I was the judge. I am a witness. I am asking you gentlemen to be the judge!

INVESTIGATOR. But there is a vast difference, apparently, between your opinion of . . . that organization and the opinion of others.

Pause.

THE CHAIRMAN. We are going to take a recess for lunch.

AFTERNOON

THE CHAIRMAN. The Committee will be in order.

MR. MANDEL. Mr. Chairman, Mr. Parks would like to talk about naming names.

THE CHAIRMAN. He expressed himself pretty fully this morning. Counsel has a few more questions. Maybe they will bring out what he wants to say.

MR. MANDEL. What he has to say is very pertinent *at this point*. I don't think we can judge it till he says it. It will take him three minutes. In view of the fact that he has cooperated so completely with the Committee, I think he should be granted three minutes!

THE CHAIRMAN. Make it as brief as you can, Mr. Parks.

MR. PARKS. I will. *Pause.* Mr. Chairman, to be a good actor, you must experience from the top of your head to the tip of your toes what you are doing. . . . As I told you, this is probably the most difficult morning and afternoon I have ever spent, and I wish that, if it were at all possible. . . . You see, it's a little different to sit *there* and to sit *here,* and if you could transfer places with me, mentally, and put yourself in my place. . . . My people have a long heritage in this country. They fought in the Revolutionary War to make this country, to create the government of which this Committee is a part. . . . I have two boys, one thirteen months, one two weeks. Is this the kind of heritage I must hand down to them? Is this the kind of heritage you would like to hand down to your children? For what purpose? . . . Children as innocent as I am or you are, people you already know. . . . I don't think I would be here today if I weren't a star, because you know

41

Larry Parks (*Associated Press*).

as well as I, even better, that I know *nothing* that would be of great service to this country. I think my career has been ruined because of this, and I would appreciate not having to— Don't present me with the choice of either being in contempt of this Committee and going to jail or being forced to crawl through the mud and be an informer! For what purpose? I don't think this is a choice at all. I don't think this is sportsmanlike. I don't think this is American. Something like that is more akin to what happened under Hitler, and what is happening in Russia. I don't think this is American justice for an innocent mistake in judgment, if it was that, with the intention behind it only of making this country a better place in which to live. . . . It is not befitting to force me to make this kind of a choice. I don't think it is befitting to *the purpose of the Committee* to do this. This is probably the most difficult thing I have ever done, and it seems to me it would impair the usefulness of this Committee. . . . God knows it is difficult enough to come before this Committee and tell the truth. . . . There was another choice open to me. I did not choose to use it. I chose to come and tell the truth. If you do this to me, it will make it almost impossible for a person to come to you, as I have done, and tell the truth. . . . I beg of you not to force me to do this!

INVESTIGATOR. Mr. Parks, there was a statement you made this morning which interested me a great deal. You said: "This is a great industry. It has an important job to do: to *call attention to certain evils*, but mainly to entertain." Now, do you believe that persons who "call attention to certain evils" ought to be dedicated to the principles of democracy as we understand them in this country?

MR. PARKS. I certainly agree!

INVESTIGATOR. Do you believe, on the other hand, that persons in those positions should be *antagonistic* to the principles of democracy, be members of a conspiracy to *overthrow* our Government?

MR. PARKS. Most assuredly I don't!

INVESTIGATOR. Then what is your opinion as to whether members of the Communist Party should be in positions of power in the various unions which control the writing of scripts, the actors, and so on?

MR. PARKS. I do *not* believe those people should be in *any* position of power!

INVESTIGATOR. Then we will ask your cooperation, before this hearing is over, in helping us ascertain those who are, or have been, members of the Communist Party. *Pause.* Now, Mr. Parks, tell us what you know of the methods by which money was raised for the Party.

MR. PARKS. I don't recall. *Pause.* I'm not trying to avoid the question!

INVESTIGATOR. I have no trick question here through which I am attempting to lead you into denial of something we know about!

MR. PARKS. I have been as aboveboard as I can! I think the testimony will bear me out! I am willing to help you, if you could be more specific! *Pause.* I have appeared at many benefits over many years—

INVESTIGATOR. Were any of these for the benefit of the Communist Party?

MR. PARKS. I don't recall any.

INVESTIGATOR. You have said you were subpoenaed because you were a star. Mr. Parks, you were subpoenaed because the Committee had information that you had knowledge about Communist activities.

MR. PARKS. All I meant was that I know nothing of any

conspiracy to overthrow this Government. And my point was that, if I were working in a drugstore, I doubt whether I would be here!

INVESTIGATOR. We have had many people before this Committee who have been engaged in very menial forms of making a livelihood.

MR. PARKS. Please don't take that in the wrong spirit!

INVESTIGATOR. I didn't fully understand your reference to the possible destruction of your career. You didn't mean to infer that this Committee was bringing you here *because* of any effect it might have on your career?

MR. PARKS. No. What I said was that, because of this, I have no career left.

INVESTIGATOR. Don't you think that question might be influenced by the fullness of the cooperation you give the Committee?

MR. PARKS. I have tried to cooperate, but I think the damage has been done.

CM 6. Don't you think the damage occurred when you became a member of an organization which advocates the overthrow of every constitutional form of government in the world? Is the Committee more to blame than your own act in affiliating with that organization? This Committee is an expression of the will of the American people.

MR. PARKS. As I told you, Congressman, when I was younger than I am now, I felt a certain way about things. I felt strongly, and I still do, about the underdog, and it was for these reasons that . . . this organization appealed to me. I later found it would not fulfill my needs. At that time, I don't even believe this was a mistake in judgment. It *may* have been. This is debatable. But my two boys, I would rather have them make the same mistake I did than not feel like making any mistake at all and be a cow in the pasture! If a man doesn't feel that way about certain things, he is not a man! I do not believe I did anything wrong!

CM 6. Mr. Parks, upon what do you base the opinion that the people whose names you have in your possession have probably severed their relations with the Communist Party?

MR. PARKS. The few people I knew are people like myself and feel the way I do.

CM 6. Well, of course, that is *your judgment* of the matter. Have you discussed Party affiliations with those with whom you were affiliated in the Party?

MR. PARKS. I have not. But these people I knew, and this is my honest opinion. And *you* know these people as well as I do.
Pause.

CM 6. In a recent case here in Washington, some of the highest officials in government testified that a man with whom they had been associated had never been a member of the Communist Party and in no way constituted any threat to our institutions. Every man who reads the newspapers now knows how fallacious that opinion was!

MR. PARKS. You know who the people are. I don't think this is American justice, to make me choose whether to be in contempt of this Committee or crawl through the mud for no purpose!

CM 6. That is problematic, Mr. Parks. I "know who they are"—*maybe* you are right, but I still think it's within the province of the Committee to determine how far they will go.

MR. PARKS. I am not setting myself up as a judge. I am asking the Committee not to make me do it.

CM 5. I think you are wrong in assuming we know all the

activities you engaged in and all the people you engaged in them with. Possibly you could furnish us with a lot of information we do not have. I feel sure you'd be willing to do that to serve the best interests of the United States.

MR. PARKS. I have told you of my activities to the best of my ability.

Pause.

THE CHAIRMAN. We will at this time make a break in the testimony. After we resume, the witness will be advised what the disposition of this Committee is with reference to his apparent disinclination to answer questions.

EVENING

The audience present during the morning and afternoon sessions is now absent. Present are only the Committee, the Investigator, Parks, and Parks's attorney.

THE CHAIRMAN. Mr. Parks, we are going to seek your co-operation in a closed session for testimony that will not be publicized until such time, if at all, as the Committee itself may deem expedient. *Pause.* Counsel will now propound additional questions.

MR. MANDEL. Is it the intention of the Committee, unless he answers these questions in private, to cite him for contempt?

THE CHAIRMAN. The Committee makes no threats.

MR. MANDEL. Just to clear his thinking, so he is fully informed of the consequences. . . .

THE CHAIRMAN. If Mr. Parks placed himself in the position of being in contempt of Congress, it is possible that the Committee may request a citation. On the other hand, it may not. Does that answer your question?

MR. MANDEL. I would like to spend another minute on it. In view of Mr. Parks's cooperative attitude—and everyone here understands what is motivating him—he feels so bad about what he has to do, and if he thought there were any chance you would elicit information that was important, he would give it to you. . . . It is only saving that little bit of something that you live with. You have to see and walk in Hollywood with that. You have to meet your children and your wife with it, your friends. . . . It is that little bit that you want to

Larry Parks (*Associated Press*).

save. Although I don't ask the Committee to commit itself, in fairness to Mr. Parks . . . he may have to sacrifice the arm with gangrene in order to save the body! He will walk around the rest of his life without an arm! I realize the purposes of this Committee, and our attitude has been one of cooperation: we want to go right through with that. Now, if this is the penalty he will have to pay, I have to urge him a different way. . . . His opinion is that what he is going to give you will only eat up his insides and you will get nothing.

THE CHAIRMAN. Mr. Attorney, the Committee is not responsible for the position he finds himself in; we are responsible for the position we find *ourselves* in.

Short pause.

INVESTIGATOR. Mr. Parks, who were the members of the cell of the Communist Party to which you were assigned?

Pause.

MR. PARKS. This is what I've been talking about. This is the thing. I am no longer fighting for myself. . . . I tell you frankly I am probably the most completely ruined man you have ever seen. I am fighting for a principle, I think, if Americanism is involved in this case. . . . This is what I have been talking about. I do not believe it befits this Committee to force me to do this. I do not believe it befits the Committee or its purposes to force me to do this. This is my honest feeling about it. I don't think it's fair play. I don't think it's in the spirit of real Americanism. They are not a danger to this country, gentlemen, the people I knew: they are people like myself.

INVESTIGATOR. Mr. Chairman, if the witness refuses to

answer the question, I see very little use in my asking him about *other* individuals.

THE CHAIRMAN. The witness has got to make up his mind. It isn't sufficient, as far as this Committee is concerned, to say that, in your opinion, it is unfair. Or un-American. The question is: Will you answer?

MR. MANDEL. I would like to ask the Chairman whether he is directing the witness to answer.

THE CHAIRMAN. The witness has been asked. He must answer or decline to answer.

MR. MANDEL. I think a little more is needed. He must be *directed* to answer, and if he refuses, just merely asking him and not going beyond, under law, is not sufficient. I think he has to be told, "You've *got* to answer."

THE CHAIRMAN. I don't understand any such rule, but, to avoid any controversy, I direct the witness to answer the question.
Pause.

MR. PARKS. I do not refuse to answer the question, but I feel that this Committee is doing a really dreadful thing! I don't believe the American people will look kindly on it!

CM 6. Mr. Parks, we are, each one of us, responsible to the American people. I, for one, resent having my duties pointed out to me!

MR. PARKS. I am not pointing your duty out.

CM 6. The inference is that we are doing something un-American. That is a personal opinion of yours. We have accountability for which we must account!

THE CHAIRMAN. The witness has said he doesn't *refuse* to answer. So I assume he is *ready* to answer.

MR. MANDEL. I think the members of the Committee are

51

all seeking to do the right thing. No question about that. In the same spirit, no one, with the heritage that Mr. Parks has to uphold, can think that he isn't as loyal as any member of this Committee. He has to do the right thing as we Americans do in our elections! Of course, when the final gong goes down, he intends to respect the will of this Committee. But he reserves the right to talk to you gentlemen and possibly *persuade* you to think differently.

THE CHAIRMAN. The Committee took the view, sir, that there might be some merit in your contention if we were still in an open hearing. But we are not.

MR. MANDEL. This is a private session, which is very considerate of the Committee, and I want to thank you. . . . *Pause.* May I have a minute to talk to Mr. Parks?

THE CHAIRMAN. Yes.

MR. MANDEL. I make this request of the Committee: I want no promise from you, just a sportsmanlike attitude, so what he gives you will not be used if it can be helped, to embarrass people in the same position he finds himself in today. . . .

THE CHAIRMAN. Nobody on this Committee has any desire to smear anyone's name.

MR. MANDEL. In the internal struggle that Mr. Park is going through, I think it would go a little lighter, having a statement from you. . . .

Mandel and Parks confer inaudibly. When they stop conferring:

INVESTIGATOR. If you will just answer the question, please. The question was: Who were the members of the Communist Party cell to which you were assigned?

A long silence.

MR. PARKS. Morris Carnovsky—

INVESTIGATOR. Will you spell that name?

MR. PARKS. I couldn't possibly spell it. Morris Carnovsky, Joe Bromberg, Sam Rossen, Anne Revere, Lee Cobb—

INVESTIGATOR. What was that name?

MR. PARKS. Lee Cobb. Gale Sondergaard, Dorothy Tree—

INVESTIGATOR. What was the name of Dorothy Tree's husband? Michael Uris?

MR. PARKS. Yes.

INVESTIGATOR. Was he a member of the cell?

MR. PARKS. Not to my knowledge.

INVESTIGATOR. Do you know whether Michael Uris was a member of the Communist Party?

MR. PARKS. I don't know.

INVESTIGATOR. Can you recall other members of that cell?

MR. PARKS. That's about all.

INVESTIGATOR. Was Howard Da Silva a member?

MR. PARKS. I don't believe I ever attended a meeting with Howard Da Silva.

INVESTIGATOR. Was Howard Da Silva a member of the Communist Party?

MR. PARKS. Not to my knowledge.

INVESTIGATOR. Was Roman Bohnen a member?

MR. PARKS. Yes.

INVESTIGATOR. He is now deceased, I believe.

MR. PARKS. He is dead.

INVESTIGATOR. Was James Cagney a member of the cell?

MR. PARKS. Not to my knowledge.

INVESTIGATOR. Was he a member of the Communist Party?

MR. PARKS. I don't recall ever hearing that he was.

INVESTIGATOR. Sam Jaffe?

MR. PARKS. I don't recall ever attending a meeting with Sam Jaffe.

Morris Carnovsky (*Wide World Photos*).

J. Edward Bromberg (*Acme Photo*).

INVESTIGATOR. Was he a member of the Communist Party?

MR. PARKS. I don't recall that Sam Jaffe was ever a member of the Communist Party.

INVESTIGATOR. John Garfield?

MR. PARKS. I don't recall ever being at a meeting with John Garfield.

INVESTIGATOR. Do you recall whether John Garfield ever addressed a Communist Party meeting?

MR. PARKS. I don't recall any such occasion.

INVESTIGATOR. Marc Lawrence, was he a member of that cell?

MR. PARKS. I believe he was.

MR. MANDEL. May I suggest to counsel, in view of the feeling of the witness—I don't mean to rush you, but this whole thing being so distasteful—I wonder if we can proceed a little faster so he doesn't suffer so much. . . .

INVESTIGATOR. I want him to be accurate. I purposely don't want to rush him in matters as important as these.

MR. MANDEL. I am just trying to be considerate of the man's feeling, doing something that—

INVESTIGATOR. I asked you this morning about Karen Morley. Was she a member of the Communist Party?

MR. PARKS. Yes.

INVESTIGATOR. Was she in this particular cell?

MR. PARKS. Yes.

INVESTIGATOR. Were lectures given in which persons outside of your cell took part?

MR. PARKS. The only one I recall was a talk by John Howard Lawson.

INVESTIGATOR. Georgia Backus, was she a member of this group?

MR. PARKS. The name doesn't ring a bell.

INVESTIGATOR. Meta Reis Rosenberg?

MR. PARKS. I don't believe I know the lady.

INVESTIGATOR. Robert Rossen?

MR. PARKS. No.

INVESTIGATOR. Philip Loeb?

MR. PARKS. I don't recall the gentleman.

INVESTIGATOR. Lloyd Gough?

MR. PARKS. Yes, I believe he was a—I saw him at a couple of meetings.

INVESTIGATOR. Sterling Hayden?

MR. PARKS. I don't recall ever being at a meeting with Sterling Hayden.

INVESTIGATOR. Will Geer?

MR. PARKS. I don't recall ever being in a meeting with Will Geer.

INVESTIGATOR. Victor Killian, Sr.?

MR. PARKS. Yes, I recall that he attended at least one meeting.

INVESTIGATOR. Victor Killian, Jr.?

MR. PARKS. I don't believe I am acquainted with the gentleman.

INVESTIGATOR. Lionel Stander?

MR. PARKS. I've met him. I don't recall attending a meeting with him.

INVESTIGATOR. Andy Devine?

MR. PARKS. I don't recall ever attending a meeting with Andy Devine.

INVESTIGATOR. Edward G. Robinson?

MR. PARKS. I don't recall ever attending a meeting with Edward G. Robinson.

INVESTIGATOR. Madeleine Carroll?

MR. PARKS. I don't recall ever attending a meeting with Madeleine Carroll

INVESTIGATOR. Gregory Peck?

MR. PARKS. I have no remembrance of attending a meeting with Gregory Peck.

INVESTIGATOR. Humphrey Bogart?

MR. PARKS. I don't recall a meeting with Humphrey Bogart.

CM 1. I think you could get some comfort out of the fact that the people mentioned have been subpoenaed. If they do appear here, it won't be as a result of anything you have testified to.

MR. PARKS. It is no comfort whatsoever.

INVESTIGATOR. Do you know of any other person whose name comes to your recollection?

MR. PARKS. I don't recall anyone else.

INVESTIGATOR. That is all, Mr. Chairman.

Pause.

CM 2. I'd like to say, Mr. Chairman, that Mr. Parks's testimony has certainly been refreshing!

CHAIRMAN. We appreciate your cooperation, Mr. Parks. You are excused.

NIGHT

Two years later, July 15, 1953, Larry Parks addressed the following letter to the Committee:

Dear Chairman Velde:
In rereading my public testimony before the House Committee on Un-American Activities, I am now convinced that it improperly reflects my true attitude. Perhaps some of the confusion in my testimony can best be explained by the fact that I was the first cooperative witness from Hollywood to appear before your Committee and at the time I was under strain. Upon reflection, I see that I did not adequately express my true beliefs—beliefs which have been even deepened and strengthened since my appearance. I wish to make it clear that I support completely the objectives of the House Committee on Un-American Activities. I believe fully that Communists and Communist intrigues should be exposed. Liberals must now embrace the cause of anti-Communism with the same dedication and zeal as we once did that of anti-Nazism. To assist your Committee in obtaining full information about the Communist Party is the duty of all who possess such evidence. If I were to testify today I would not testify as I did in 1951—that to give such testimony is to "wallow in the mud"—on the contrary, I would recognize that such cooperation would help the cause. My statement about not wanting my sons to become "cows in the pasture" needs clarification. I want my sons to participate in the search for democratic answers to the threat of totalitarianism. I hope the Committee will publish the statement of my militant anti-Communist beliefs at the earliest possible date. If there is any way in which I can further aid in exposing

the methods of entrapment and deceit through which Communist conspirators have gained the adherence of American liberals, I hope the Committee will so advise me.

Sincerely,
Larry Parks.

On September 19, 1951, the Chairman stated:

There can be no odium attached to persons who have made a mistake and seek to rectify it. If there was, we would give the lie to the advent of Jesus Christ in this world, who came here for the purpose of making possible forgiveness upon repentance.

The screenwriter Nicholas Bela told the Committee:

I want to humbly apologize for the grave error which I have committed, and beg of you to forgive me. I feel, if I am allowed, I would like to stand.

And he stood.

On April 10, 1951, Sterling Hayden came before the Committee.

INVESTIGATOR. After your return to Hollywood in 1946, did you become associated with any organizations?

MR. HAYDEN. I joined the Communist Party.

INVESTIGATOR. You joined the Communist Party?

MR. HAYDEN. Yes.

INVESTIGATOR. Will you tell the Committee the circumstances?

MR. HAYDEN. I was put in contact with a woman, Bea Winters.

INVESTIGATOR. How do you spell Bea?

MR. HAYDEN. B, e, a. I wanted to do something for a better world. If I could do something about the condition of the world, I could probably justify my position as an actor with a good salary and good working conditions. As I began to operate around Hollywood, I continued to talk, almost incessantly, about this thing built up in me by the Partisans in Yugoslavia—

INVESTIGATOR. What was the character of your work with the Partisans of Yugoslavia?

MR. HAYDEN. We established a close personal feeling with these people. Had unlimited respect for the way they were fighting. Our plane crews would leave their *shoes* with the Partisans, they were that impressed. It had a strong emotional impact. *Pause.* Bea Winters said, "Why don't you stop talking and join the Communist Party?" She had a paper, which I signed.

INVESTIGATOR. Did you have an assignment from the Communist Party in Hollywood?

MR. HAYDEN. I was told it would be helpful if the Screen Actors Guild could be swung into line in support of

Sterling Hayden (*Acme Photo*).

a strike. So I went to a large cocktail party, and began to meet actors and actresses who felt the same way.

INVESTIGATOR. You have given a list of persons to the investigators of this Committee, have you not?

MR. HAYDEN. I have.

INVESTIGATOR. Are there any you can identify as members of the Communist Party?

MR. HAYDEN. I wouldn't hesitate to say Karen Morley.

INVESTIGATOR. Did Karen Morley meet with you?

MR. HAYDEN. Yes.

INVESTIGATOR. Where were these meetings held?

MR. HAYDEN. Some at her house, some at a house owned by Morris Carnovsky.

INVESTIGATOR. You have told the investigators what you have known of Communism. Have you taken any other action which would indicate good faith in the break you claim you have made?

MR. HAYDEN. One month after South Korea was invaded, my attorney sent a letter to J. Edgar Hoover, in which—

INVESTIGATOR. Suppose you read that letter.

MR. HAYDEN, *reading.*

Dear Sir,

In June of 1946, in a moment of emotional disturbance, a young man became a member of the Communist Party. In November he decided he had made a mistake and terminated his membership. Ever since, this client of ours has had no connection with the Communist Party. He is an American-born citizen with a distinguished war record. He enlisted in the Marine Corps as a private and received his termination as a captain. He received the Silver Star medal with citation from the commanding general. Since Korea, our client has felt that the time may come when his services might be of aid to the United States. He is concerned with the fact that his brief membership in the Communist Party may prevent the use of his services. He is married and has young children. If his services are not needed by the United States, conditions may require an answer, in connection with ordinary employment, to the query: 'Are you now, or have you ever been, a Communist?' Our client can answer that he is not now a member of the Communist Party. He could not answer the rest of the question without either lying, or, if he told the truth, finding himself unable to earn a living. Justice requires some method by which one mistake does not operate (a) to prevent the United States from making use of our client, (b) to prevent our client from earning a living. He is willing to submit to interrogation by the FBI. The purpose of this is to permit our client, if the question is asked, to say, 'Please inquire of the FBI.' The FBI could then notify the prospective employer that there was no reason for not employing our client.

INVESTIGATOR. Was a reply received?
MR. HAYDEN. Yes. *He reads.*

Dear Sir:
It is considered advisable that your client furnish our Los Angeles Office with details concerning his membership in the Communist Party. I suggest that you contact Mr. R. B. Hood, special agent in charge of our Los Angeles office.

Very truly yours,
John Edgar Hoover.

INVESTIGATOR. Did you report as requested?
MR. HAYDEN. Yes.

INVESTIGATOR. Now, I asked you to name members of the Communist Party in the Screen Actors Guild and you named those you knew?

MR. HAYDEN. I did.

INVESTIGATOR. You indicated that you could name others. Have you given the investigators of this Committee a list of those?

MR. HAYDEN. Yes.

THE CHAIRMAN. Upon some conjecture that they *may* have been members of the Party?

MR. HAYDEN. That is true.

THE CHAIRMAN. Your purpose in furnishing the list of names was that, by proper investigation, their connection with the Communist Party might be revealed?

MR. HAYDEN. I think it would be developed.

Pause.

INVESTIGATOR. Have you anything to add, Mr. Hayden?

MR. HAYDEN. I would like to say I appreciate very much, very, *very* much, the opportunity to appear here today. I think there is a service to be rendered, not only to the country at large but to those who find themselves in a similar position to mine. I have heard there are hundreds of thousands of ex-Communists who don't know what to do about it. The suggestion made by the Chairman of this Committee that people come up and speak is extremely fine, constructive. My appearance before this Committee could serve a very useful purpose!

In an autobiography published later, Sterling Hayden writes of telling his psychiatrist about his appearance before the Committee:

If it hadn't been for you, I wouldn't have turned into a stoolie for J. Edgar Hoover. I don't think you have the foggiest notion of the contempt I have had for myself since the day I did that thing. Fuck it! And fuck you too! I'd like to take a two-page spread in the *Hollywood Reporter* and *Variety* and let go the goddamnedest blast—let people know who the *real* subversives are!

On April 25, 1951, Edward Dmytryk came before the Committee for the second time.

MR. DMYTRYK. The situation has changed.

INVESTIGATOR. What do you mean by that?

MR. DMYTRYK. Before '47 I had never heard anybody say they would refuse to fight for this country in a war against Soviet Russia. Then I saw articles about Party members taking that position: I believe Paul Robeson was one. I signed the Stockholm Peace Petition, along with other people. I hoped they were sincere. The Korean War made me realize they were not. The North Koreans would not have attacked the South Koreans unless they had the backing of very strong forces: those forces are China and Russia. This made me realize there is a Communist menace, and that the Communist Party in this country is a part of that menace. The next thing was the spy trials, the Hiss, Coplon, and Greenglass cases, the Klaus Fuchs case. This is treason. I don't say all Communists are guilty of treason, but I think a Party that encourages them to act in this capacity is treasonable. For this reason I am willing to talk.

INVESTIGATOR. I would like to have you state what the real object of the Communist Party is in Hollywood.

MR. DMYTRYK. They had three purposes: to get money, to get prestige, and to control the content of pictures. The only way they could control the content of pictures was to take over the guilds and the unions.

INVESTIGATOR. What information do you have regarding money?

MR. DMYTRYK. There was the opportunity to hold a great many affairs—parties, dinners, meetings of various sorts. When the love feast was on between Russia and

Edward Dmytryk (*Acme Photo*).

America during the war, a great deal of money was taken from Hollywood.

INVESTIGATOR. You referred to prestige?

MR. DMYTRYK. They were able to approach name people in Hollywood and get their names on resolutions or as members of the boards of Communist fronts. The Communists are tireless workers. One tireless worker can take over. A Communist doesn't want to be president. He wants to be secretary. As secretary he takes control.

INVESTIGATOR. What guilds were they that you referred to?

MR. DMYTRYK. The Communists were successful for a time in controlling the Screen Writers Guild. They were not successful in the Screen Directors Guild.

INVESTIGATOR. How many people were there in the Screen Directors Guild?

MR. DMYTRYK. 230.

INVESTIGATOR. And of that number there were a few Communists?

MR. DMYTRYK. Seven.

INVESTIGATOR. Will you give us the names?

MR. DMYTRYK. Frank Tuttle, Herbert Biberman, Jack Berry, he's the Berry who lives on King's Road, Bernard Vorhaus, Jules Dassin, and myself.

INVESTIGATOR. Do you know the names of individuals in the Screen *Writers* Guild who were Communists?

MR. DMYTRYK. John Howard Lawson, Lester Cole, Gordon Kahn. . . .

INVESTIGATOR. Tell us the circumstances of your joining.

MR. DMYTRYK. About this time, 1943, the People's Educational Center was organized. One of the classes was in screen direction, I became one of the lecturers. I learned the Communists were running the organization, but I didn't say "How horrible," I said, "The Communists are doing something good." I was approached by people to join the Party. I was curious. So I agreed to go to a recruiting meeting.

INVESTIGATOR. Who asked you to?

MR. DMYTRYK. Alvah Bessie, later one of the Hollywood Ten. He spoke at the meeting.

INVESTIGATOR. Who were the others in that group?

MR. DMYTRYK. Lester Cole. A man named Sackin. The others I don't know; you aren't introduced by your last name. Later I moved to Beverly Hills. In that group I saw Herbert Biberman, Arnold Manoff, Mickey Uris, Leonardo Bercovici. . . .

INVESTIGATOR. Then you were transferred to another group?

MR. DMYTRYK. A special group: John Howard Lawson, Adrian Scott, Francis Faragoh, his wife Elizabeth, and myself.

Pause.

INVESTIGATOR. Mr. Dmytryk, I understand you learned a good deal about Communism through your association with the Hollywood Ten?

MR. DMYTRYK. We held affairs to collect money, functions, dinners, that sort of thing. Speeches were made. I made a couple myself. . . . But I couldn't work in Hollywood: we were fired, those of us who were under contract, five out of the Ten. . . . I went to England to make a couple of pictures and came back when it was assumed our case would get up to the Supreme Court and we would either go to jail or not. We had a great many meetings of the Ten. A change had taken place while I was gone. The group was now following the Party line all the way. I argued that we ought to include as many people as we could, middle-of-the-roaders, everybody. However, the group put stuff out in defense of the New York Eleven, the Harry Bridges case, every case that came up. Sometimes others would agree with my point of view, but when the argument got hot, somebody could call on John Howard Lawson and then on Ben Margolis, and the dialectical reasoning would come, and the Party-line dictate would come.

INVESTIGATOR. Was there any indication in '47 that the Communist Party was endeavoring to influence the course of action you as a group should take?

MR. DMYTRYK. The answer would probably be yes, but we went into it not realizing. We came back to Washington and had a large suite at the Shoreham Hotel—

INVESTIGATOR. Did any person appear to discuss matters?

MR. DMYTRYK. Two persons. One was Lee Pressman, who delivered a little speech.

INVESTIGATOR. What was the subject?

MR. DMYTRYK. We were in the forefront of a battle for freedom, we were on the barricades. The other was Harry Bridges.

INVESTIGATOR. Did you gain the impression your group was being *encouraged* by Lee Pressman and Harry Bridges in the stand it was taking?

MR. DMYTRYK. There was no question about that.

INVESTIGATOR. Well, the result of your agreement was you would refuse to testify?

MR. DMYTRYK. Yes. We were fighting it on the First Amendment. Since we believed the procedures of the Committee were not proper, the only way to test it was to take them into court, or have them take us into court—which is what happened—on a constitutional issue. We were sure we would be cited for contempt, and we believed we could get a Supreme Court decision in our favor.

INVESTIGATOR. Mr. Dmytryk, when do you consider you withdrew from the Communist Party?

MR. DMYTRYK. In the fall of '45. However, I was teaching at the Center till '47. I was on the board of the Arts, Sciences, and Professions Council. I was a member of the Hollywood Ten. So I *didn't* break. I want to explain that. As a man who'd made his choice in his appearance before the Committee in '47, I felt I should follow this choice until the Supreme Court either decided we were right—or we were wrong and went to jail. I felt, if I started crying uncle, I was doing it to avoid going to jail, although I'd already made up my mind, as soon as my sentence was over, I'd issue an affidavit and disclose that I'd been a member of the Party. Actually, I issued such an affidavit while in prison, the Korean War so bothered me.

INVESTIGATOR. To whom did you give this affidavit?

MR. DMYTRYK. Two attorneys. In the presence of the superintendent of Mill Point Prison. *Pause.* I've heard rumors. One, that I'd been offered a job at M-G-M at five thousand a week if I would make such an affidavit. The other is, "They put the works to Dmytryk in jail, they put the pressure on him, and *that's* why he made his affidavit." There was no pressure, nor have I ever been offered a bribe or a job—I wish I had!

INVESTIGATOR. This was a statement dictated by your own conscience?

MR. DMYTRYK. Absolutely.

Pause.

CM 1. Mr. Dmytryk, it is refreshing to find there are people who are willing to assist our feeble efforts to make a contribution in this world-wide struggle against Communism. I think you have made a very great contribution.

MR. DMYTRYK. Thank you.

CM 2. What would you call the final test of credibility of a witness purporting to be a former Communist? Primarily the willingness to name names?

MR. DMYTRYK. I believe so. That is why I am doing it. I know there have been comments that people who talk are informers. I went to the dictionary and looked up the word. An informer is a man who informs against colleagues who are engaged in criminal activity. By using this word, the Communists are admitting they are engaged in criminal activity!

THE CHAIRMAN. Permit me, Mr. Dmytryk, to add my feeble expression of appreciation for your coming here, and for the information you have given the American people, millions of whom haven't the vaguest conception what the Communist movement stands for!

The Hollywood director Frank Tuttle testified:

There is a traditional dislike among Americans for informers, and I am an informer. The aggressors are ruthless, and I feel it is absolutely necessary for Americans to be ruthless.

The Hollywood director Robert Rossen testified:

I don't feel I'm being a stool pigeon or an informer, that is rather romantic, like children playing at cops and robbers. . . . I don't think any one individual can indulge himself in the luxury of individual morality or pit it against the security and safety of this nation.

On July 13, 1951 *Hollywood Life* carried the headline: DORE SCHARY AND DASHIELL HAMMETT, COMMUNIST CONNECTIONS
Earlier that year they had run the headline:
JOHN GARFIELD LENA HORNE JUDY HOLLIDAY JOSÉ FERRER HOWARD DUFF ORSON WELLES SUPPORT COMMUNIST PARTY

In testifying before the Un-American Activities Committee, John Garfield said the Communist Party should be outlawed so that people like him would be protected from it. José Ferrer, who had celebrated May Day without knowing what May Day celebrated, and who had helped elect Communist Councilman Ben Davis without knowing Davis's party, was propelled by the Committee on May 22, 1951 toward certain conclusions.

INVESTIGATOR. Do you have any suggestions, Mr. Ferrer, about Communist-front organizations in your profession?
MR. FERRER. It is extremely important that the ability of this Committee rapidly to inform any member of the

José Ferrer (*Acme Photo*).

profession who wants instruction be highly publicized! This service exists, but I don't think the people know about it. I think that if they knew we can go in and find out, we have a place that is set up to keep us out of this trouble . . . next to making it illegal, the Communist Party and all Communist activity—which would be the biggest help of all—some kind of a center where people who want help can get it, can receive a welcome when they come asking questions. . . . There is nothing like dragging something out into the open and exposing it to air!

CM 1. That is what this Committee has been doing for years, and you didn't believe it until a few days ago.

CM 2. Mr. Ferrer, what course of action could this Committee take in advertising that May Day is an international Communist celebration?

MR. FERRER. I think that is no longer necessary.

CM 2. What course can we take, as far as artists are concerned, in instances where they support Communist candidates for public office?

MR. FERRER. We have all learned a lot in the last few months, sir. I certainly have. If the question ever comes up before me, I am going to very strongly advise people to find out, tell them this Committee exists and they should—

CM 1. Why wait until the question comes before you? Why not start now?

MR. FERRER. Mr. Kearney, if you tell me how, I will be glad to. I will. I'll ask you for a few suggestions! If it comes up in conversation with younger members in the theater, newcomers that I come in contact with. . . . They say, "Joe, how did you make out today? What are you going to do in the future?" I'll tell

77

José Ferrer (*Acme Photo*).

them! The youth, who are the tomorrow of the theater, *there* is where we can be useful!

CM 2. Do I understand, Mr. Ferrer, that you advocate the outlawing of the Communist Party?

MR. FERRER. Yes, sir, I do! Definitely! Emphatically!

CM 2. Would you assign a reason *why* it should be outlawed?

MR. FERRER. Because, through conversations, investigation, and research I have done, because of the subpoena and my appearance here, I have been convinced, and it has been pointed out to me irrefutably, that the Communist Party of America is the instrument, definitely, of a foreign government, that its aims are those of a foreign government, and have nothing to do with our own life or our own welfare. The mere fact that it is un-American seems to me to make it *ipso facto* illegal!

Before the end of 1951 Ronald Reagan proclaimed a victory:

For many years the Red propagandists and conspirators concentrated their big guns on Hollywood. They threatened to throw acid in the faces of myself and some other stars, so we would never appear on screen again. I packed a gun for some time. Policemen lived at my home to guard my kids. But that was more than five years ago. Those days are gone forever!

Part Two

1952. *Guys and Dolls,* already a Broadway hit, had been optioned for the movies by Paramount. They had paid $75,000 for their option when it turned out that one of the authors and owners of the work, Abe Burrows, had a past.

INVESTIGATOR. Mr. Burrows, you appeared in executive session of this Committee in 1951. Your testimony was *vague* with regard to individuals who have been members of the Communist Party. The investigation has continued. There was a witness in 1952, Mr. Owen Vinson, who testified, "Abe Burrows attended meetings of the Communist Party which I attended, yes, sir." Upon taking this testimony, we heard that you desired to appear before this Committee.

MR. BURROWS. The first time I was subpoenaed by this Committee I got in touch with my lawyer instantly and we asked to come down as quickly as possible. That was March '51. I was frightened. I'd been around in an atmosphere of people who disliked this Committee, and I knew nothing about it except some of the stuff I had heard, and there had been a lot of—well, I might use the word "propaganda." But I came down here and spoke to the investigators. There were no monsters here, no Fascists, nobody trying to kill me. The minute I heard Vinson had said something about me,

Abe Burrows (*UPI*).

I wanted to come back and talk to you people again because I really want to get this thing cleared up. My Americanism being under suspicion is very painful to me, not just economically but painful to a guy who loves his country, his home, his people. I have no recollection of ever applying for Party membership, although I've been told that somebody had seen a card with my name on it. I've never seen such a card and I don't believe it. I have no recollection of paying dues. I have no recollection of any formal participation. However, I did associate with Communists. I went to meetings, I belonged to a lot of their fronts, I attended lectures, what was called study groups or something, I entertained for their causes, I gave them money for these causes. And so, if someone testifies that he thought I was a Communist, I guess he's telling the truth as he sees it. However, kind of a stubborn pride on my part makes me happy in the belief that maybe I didn't take the final step.

INVESTIGATOR. By "final step," what do you mean?

MR. BURROWS. I mean the actual going through the ritualistic stuff which you had to go through before you became a member.

CM 1. Did you attend Communist cell meetings?

MR. BURROWS. Back in '43, I met a fellow named Samuel Sillen. We met in the country or somewhere, and started to talk books. He introduced me to Joe North, who was managing editor of the *New Masses,* and another fellow named John Stewart, I think it was, and they would sit around and talk to me. At one time they said, "You ought to be much closer to us." When I came to California, about a week after I arrived, I was called by Albert Maltz, and Maltz said, "Samuel Sillen said for me to get in touch with you." He came with his wife and visited me at my home.

CM 2. Was Samuel Sillen a member of the Communist Party?

MR. BURROWS. Well, sir, he was literary editor of the *New Masses*.

CM 2. And Joe North, did you know *him* to be a member?

MR. BURROWS. He would say, "We Communists." *Pause.* They once invited me to a lecture under the auspices of the Communist Party in which Earl Browder had a debate with George Sokolsky! Everybody got along in those days! '43. A big crowd and stuff like that.

CM 2. How about John Stewart? Did you know him to be a member of the Communist Party?

MR. BURROWS. Well, he wrote a book with a fellow who used to give lectures in Hollywood on the Marxist approach to history or something. Everything was called things like that, you know. A fellow named Bruce Minton.

CM 2. Do you know whether Bruce Minton used any other name?

MR. BURROWS. His real name was Richard Bransten, I believe.

CM 2. How well did you know him?

MR. BURROWS. I was at his home a couple of times. His wife was Ruth McKenney. . . . In those days, I was invited everywhere. Attended more parties than anyone. The *Saturday Evening Post* did an article about me and the fact that I played at parties all over Hollywood. It got a little out of hand, I used to go to too many, and, when I started to get asked by people I didn't know, I began to quit going. You know, people would say, "Come to the party," so I attended parties, with all kinds of people, right, left, middle. I never turned down an invitation to go to the piano, I played up these songs!

CM 2. Now, as to these study groups, you studied Communism?

MR. BURROWS. To orientate people on what they called a Marxist approach to show business. They used to have continual squabbles as to the role of a writer. If you recall, it was a tremendous controversy that Albert Maltz had, I think it was, where he said art is a weapon, and they said art isn't a weapon. Or rather he said art *isn't* a weapon, and they said it *is* a weapon. I used to find myself in arguments. . . . I'm a satirist, and one of my best-known satires is a satire of a kind of documentary radio program that was very common among the left-wing writers of the day. There was a big tendency to do these very pontifical radio programs with everybody talking very loud and introducing Thomas Jefferson and Abraham Lincoln. So I did a thing on that at the piano. The first time I did it was for some kind of a cause, and there was a pretty large left-wing crowd, I guess, and there was a kind of a quiet in the room, and then one of the fellows came over, I think it was Henry Blankfort, and said, "That is a very bad thing for you to do, Abe, you know." I said, "Why?" and he said, "Because I think it is wrong." These guys had no sense of humor about themselves. That's one of the reasons I wasn't too trusted.

CM 2. Did you know Henry Blankfort as a member of the Communist Party?

MR. BURROWS. I knew he testified and took the Fifth Amendment. In some cases, I don't know whether I know a fellow was a Communist from reading about it in this Committee's testimony or whether I knew it before! It kind of overlaps in your mind, you know!

CM 2. Do you recall any of these study groups?

MR. BURROWS. One of them was the group Bruce Minton ran. It was called a study group, but he just talked. Engaged in a terrific controversy with John Howard Lawson over how history was to be interpreted. I didn't know what either of them meant. That was one group. Then there was a book called *Literature and Arts,* by Marx and Engels, or something. And a group gathered to discuss this. A lot of the people were kind of faceless to me, and when I saw the list that Owen Vinson named as the group I was supposed to have been part of, I knew, maybe, two of them.

CM 2. Mr. Burrows, you are a fairly intelligent man. Couldn't you tell from the way their Party line shifted that you were studying Marxist Communism?

MR. BURROWS. Oh, yes, I knew that—

CM 2. And if you were interested in Marxist Communism, don't you think it's reasonable to assume you were a member of the Communist Party?

MR. BURROWS. The study groups I mentioned, Mr. Velde, were in '45, when there was no word of Marxist Communism as we know it. It was a case of the writers' role in the war, in establishing unity, how the writer should treat minorities, the war effort, he shouldn't make jokes about gas rationing, stuff like that. I attended no such study groups when the Party switched back to a revolutionary role!

CM 2. But you know, don't you, that to get into those study groups, you had to be considered for membership in the Communist Party?

MR. BURROWS. Well, because of my work, my humor, my satire, I wasn't very well trusted. I was called chi-chi because I did satires on folk songs in a period when the Communist Party had taken the folk song very dearly to its bosom.

THE CHAIRMAN. During the period '43 to '45 what was your annual income?

MR. BURROWS. In '43, about $40,000, in '44 about $50,000, in '45 over $50,000.

THE CHAIRMAN. Can you name organizations you contributed to?

MR. BURROWS. Hollywood Independent Citizens Committee. I once gave money to a *People's World* fund.

THE CHAIRMAN. You knew what you were doing?

MR. BURROWS. Yes, sir.

THE CHAIRMAN. You know where the money was going to?

MR. BURROWS. To the *People's World* fund, yes, sir.

INVESTIGATOR. And the *New Masses?*

MR. BURROWS. Yes, sir.

THE CHAIRMAN. You knew where that was going?

MR. BURROWS. Yes, sir.

THE CHAIRMAN. All right, then, categorically, did you pay dues to the Communist Party?

MR. BURROWS. Not to my knowledge, sir.

THE CHAIRMAN. Categorically, were you ever requested to pay dues to the Communist Party as such?

MR. BURROWS. Not to my knowledge, sir.

THE CHAIRMAN. Categorically, did you ever decline to pay dues because you didn't have the money with you?

MR. BURROWS. Well, categorically, no, sir. Because it just doesn't sound like me.

THE CHAIRMAN. I'm not asking what it sounds like. Did you or did you not?

MR. BURROWS. No, sir.

THE CHAIRMAN. Did you ever give Owen Vinson any money for any purpose?

MR. BURROWS. I may have, sir.

THE CHAIRMAN. Do you know whether you did or not?

MR. BURROWS. I couldn't answer that for sure, sir.

THE CHAIRMAN. Now, categorically, when he said that you paid him money for Communist Party dues, was he telling the truth?

MR. BURROWS. He may have thought he was telling the truth.

THE CHAIRMAN. I didn't ask you that.

MR. BURROWS. It is very difficult for me to say, because—

THE CHAIRMAN. Did you pay Vinson Communist Party dues, as he swore before this Committee?

MR. BURROWS. No, sir, not to my knowledge.

Pause.

INVESTIGATOR. Mr. Vinson told us he was a member of that group of radio writers, and named other persons. You stated you knew two of them. Who were the two?

MR. BURROWS. Sam Moore and Georgia Backus.

INVESTIGATOR. Did you know Sam Moore to be a member of the Communist Party?

MR. BURROWS. He was active in a lot of these Communist things, and he seemed to be always around.

INVESTIGATOR. Have you had any conversation with Sam Moore with regard to testifying?

MR. BURROWS. Yes, sir. I got the subpoena, got in touch with my lawyer, and we agreed to ask for an immediate hearing in Washington, well in advance of the date we were called. Sam called me up—I hadn't seen him for a number of years—and said he'd like to see me. We met at Moore's restaurant right next to the 48th Street Theater where I was rehearsing. Sam said, "I hear you got a subpoena." I said, "Yep," and he said, "I got one, too." I hadn't known that, it wasn't in the paper. He said, "What are you going to do with it?" I said, "Well, I have to keep that to myself." He said, "Well, the only thing to do is to stick with the Fifth

Amendment." I said, "Sam, it is something I don't agree with you on, but I can't argue with you." It got very cold in the restaurant and I got up. As a matter of fact, we ordered coffee and I didn't finish the coffee. I paid the bill and went to my rehearsal, and he left, and I haven't seen him since.

THE CHAIRMAN. Why would he ask you to avail yourself of the Fifth Amendment?

MR. BURROWS. His theory was everybody ought to stick together.

THE CHAIRMAN. Everybody?

MR. BURROWS. Everybody!

INVESTIGATOR. Was Georgia Backus known to you to be a member of the Communist Party?

MR. BURROWS. I kind of assumed it. She was very intense about everything.

INVESTIGATOR. Do you recall meetings at which she was present?

MR. BURROWS. Yes. Georgia was at everything.

INVESTIGATOR. Who acted as a chairman?

MR. BURROWS. I don't recall.

INVESTIGATOR. Were you acquainted with Hy Alexander?

MR. BURROWS. Slightly.

INVESTIGATOR. Was *he* chairman?

MR. BURROWS. He wasn't the type. A very quiet fellow. I think he was married to Georgia Backus. He was married to somebody.

CM 2. Mr. Burrows, have you never signed an application for the Communist Party?

MR. BURROWS. Not to my knowledge, sir. I think I'd remember.

CM 2. Are you equally sure you never signed your name on a Party card?

MR. BURROWS. Yes, sir. As I said, somebody told me they saw a card with my name on it. I don't know how anybody would have a card that I signed.

THE CHAIRMAN. Do you sign instruments without knowing what they are?

MR. BURROWS. No, sir.

THE CHAIRMAN. You read what you sign?

MR. BURROWS. Yes, sir.

THE CHAIRMAN. Then why are you indefinite about whether you signed it?

MR. BURROWS. I am not indefinite.

THE CHAIRMAN. You say now, categorically, you did not do it?

MR. BURROWS. To my recollection, I never signed any such thing.

THE CHAIRMAN. That is still indefinite. Will you tell us whether you signed?

MR. BURROWS. No, sir.

THE CHAIRMAN. You did not do it?

MR. BURROWS. I have no recollection of doing such a thing.

THE CHAIRMAN. I asked you *did* you do it.

MR. BURROWS. Well, I say, sir—

THE CHAIRMAN. Do you want to leave the Committee in doubt?

MR. BURROWS. No, sir.

THE CHAIRMAN. Then did you?

MR. BURROWS. I didn't.

THE CHAIRMAN. Proceed, Mr. Tavenner.
    Pause.

INVESTIGATOR. When did these discussions regarding literature take place?

MR. BURROWS. Somebody would say, "A group of us are getting together for a talkfest Monday night," or something.

INVESTIGATOR. Who would notify you?

MR. BURROWS. Well, I would get a card, which would say, at so forth and so forth, literature and art is going to be discussed. . . .

INVESTIGATOR. In whose homes were these meetings held?

MR. BURROWS. A lot of them were held in places that didn't seem to be homes. They seemed to be houses but not homes. They were sparsely furnished. I remember one on the Crescent Heights Boulevard or something. Nobody seemed to live there. I remember Vinson's house because he was the one who put up the chairs. You figure it's the host who's doing that.

INVESTIGATOR. Were you acquainted with Elizabeth Glenn?

MR. BURROWS. I met her. She used to kind of wheel around at benefits and big functions. She seemed to be a person of some authority.

INVESTIGATOR. She was a functionary of the Communist Party.

MR. BURROWS. She was an exceptionally large lady. A lot of these people on the Left would show up at my place, and she was brought one night by Richard Bransten. Bruce Minton.

INVESTIGATOR. What was the purpose of her visit?

MR. BURROWS. They dropped by after some kind of thing, where everybody dropped by at somebody's house for a drink, and I knew him, and I guess I told him to drop by for a drink. After a rally or something. She was engaged at the time. She said, "Did you read Albert Maltz's new book?" Maltz had just written *The Cross and the Arrow,* I think it was, a book about war in Germany, and I said, "No," and she said it was terrible.

INVESTIGATOR. Did you know she was a functionary of the Communist Party?

MR. BURROWS. I assumed she was a wheel.

INVESTIGATOR. Were you acquainted with Elaine Gonda?

MR. BURROWS. I remembered her when I read Charles Glenn's name because they were having a romance or something. It struck me, because I remember them sitting—

INVESTIGATOR. Well, they became married, didn't they?

MR. BURROWS. Really? Well, that's the end of the romance.

INVESTIGATOR. That was Elaine Gonda.

MR. BURROWS. They used to sit and hold hands!

Pause.

INVESTIGATOR. You met Samuel Sillen in New York. When *was* that?

MR. BURROWS. 1943. A very bright fellow. I found him good company. And he introduced me to these other people from the *New Masses,* and they asked me to their houses, and we had seven or eight sessions of talk. They said they hadn't had a humor column for a long time. You know there wasn't anything very humorous in the *New Masses.* So Joe North asked me would I consider doing a humor column. And I said no.

INVESTIGATOR. Why?

MR. BURROWS. I never wrote for a Communist publication!

INVESTIGATOR. But, if you would associate with all these Communists, if you would contribute to the support of the *People's World* and the *New Masses* . . . ?

MR. BURROWS. I never went all the way.

INVESTIGATOR. You don't admit having been a member of the Communist Party, but you do admit—?

MR. BURROWS. When the Chairman questioned me today, I got a sharp insight. It hit me like a flash when he said, "Why did Sam Moore come to you?" I had never asked myself, *Why* did he come to me? *Sam Moore thought I was a member, or he* wouldn't *have come to me.*

92

INVESTIGATOR. Sam Moore had a *right* to think you were a member?

MR. BURROWS. The people I was around with could have *thought* I was a member. My sloppiness or whatever it was gave them the right to think I was.

INVESTIGATOR. Were you an instructor at the People's Educational Center, Mr. Burrows?

MR. BURROWS. I was.

INVESTIGATOR. Who solicited you for that work?

MR. BURROWS. The executive director. Kenneth, I think. I don't know the whole name. He said to me, "We want to have a class in radio comedy writing, how would you like to do it?" I said, "I'll take a whack at it." Is there a name Kenneth something?
Pause.

INVESTIGATOR. There may be a number of people by that name.
Pause.

MR. BURROWS. I kind of enjoyed it for a little while. I was the kind of guy who loved to pop off.

INVESTIGATOR. Were you affiliated with the Joint Anti-Fascist Refugee Committee?

MR. BURROWS. I don't know. Somebody called me and said, "Abe, would you do a benefit Saturday night?" I do thousands of things. But now I watch them.

INVESTIGATOR. When did you begin *watching* them?

MR. BURROWS. Right after the war, when the Communist Party was opposed to building up American defenses, I did a whole series of radio shows for the United States Army. I recruited soldiers and Marines, wrote the shows, prepared them, and put them on for the Army! I got a citation from the Army for it! And I have this letter from the Poor Richard Club of Philadelphia: "The directors of the Poor Richard Club are gratified to learn that you have consented to join the club in honoring General Eisenhower at the Bellevue-Stratford Hotel, January 17."

INVESTIGATOR. What year?

MR. BURROWS. 1948. With General Eisenhower at this thing! I was thrilled! I went to the dinner. That was the time they started the big Republican move for Eisenhower. . . .

CM 2. You recall the days when the White House was picketed by Communist Party members, don't you?

MR. BURROWS. Oh, that was during the Nazi-Soviet pact, '39 to '41. When I got with these fellows, they were all sweetness and light, '43, because my stand, on Communism itself never changed. I am kind of anti-authoritarian in my thinking. I hate their whole approach, that says any means to an end is O.K.!

CM 2. Were you conscious of the fact that the Party line was directed from Russia?

MR. BURROWS. I was, during the pact, sir.

CM 2. Up to June 21, 1941, you were conscious that policy was directed by Russia?

MR. BURROWS. I was.

CM 2. After that you *weren't* conscious of it?

MR. BURROWS. To my eternal regret, I was sucked back in. Somehow or other I got sucked in by all the statements about unity.

CM 2. Tell me about your feeling at the time you got sucked back in.

MR. BURROWS. My feeling was they were sincere. They were an American-directed party acting on their own.

CM 2. I must say, Mr. Burrows, you were pretty naïve.

MR. BURROWS. I would say I was *stupid*. I could never go along with revolution. Violence. I hate dictatorship.

They tell you the means are justified by the end. I don't believe that. I don't believe you kill people for their own good. All you do by killing people is make the world nonexistent. I want to fight Communism, prove how much I hate this whole thing! I can fight it best with my own weapons. An anti-Communist comedy—

INVESTIGATOR. Our observation has been that ridicule is one of the most effective weapons against the Communist Party!

MR. BURROWS. They can't take it. I read somewhere they don't like jokes. Stalin likes an opera to be serious!

THE CHAIRMAN. I'll ask you the question now: are you a member of the Communist Party?

MR. BURROWS. No, sir.

THE CHAIRMAN. Have you ever been a member of the Communist Party?

MR. BURROWS. I've never applied for membership. If there's a Party card with my name, I know nothing about it.

THE CHAIRMAN. Answer that question whether you have ever been, or considered yourself, a member of the Communist Party.

MR. BURROWS. I was *considered* a Communist.

THE CHAIRMAN. You so considered yourself?

MR. BURROWS. In my own heart, I didn't, but I was considered a Communist, and that was the whole thing of my coming here.

THE CHAIRMAN. You know whether or not you were, don't you?

MR. BURROWS. Well, you see, sir, I committed enough acts to be *called* a Communist. . . .

THE CHAIRMAN. Would you have called yourself a Communist?

MR. BURROWS. Not in my own heart, sir. But I'm here to

tell the truth, the whole truth, and nothing but the truth, and there's an element of truth in the statement that I was a Communist. *Pause.* There's also an element of untruth.

THE CHAIRMAN. Were you ever a member of the Communist Party?

MR. BURROWS. Well, sir . . . I don't deny the truth of the accusations of the witness.

THE CHAIRMAN. I can't understand how you can say you are not *now* a member of the Communist Party, and not clearly express whether you have *ever* been.

MR. BURROWS. I was around with those fellows. I did go to meetings with them. I *was,* by association—by association, sir! I can't deny that under oath!

THE CHAIRMAN. Well, that's the point. You're not necessarily a Communist by association. I mean you *were* not.

MR. BURROWS. I say they *assumed* me to be one, and I'm not denying they had a right to.

THE CHAIRMAN. You mean you participated in Communist activities with a reservation in your heart?

MR. BURROWS. Yes, sir. That is very well put.

CM 2. You did attend Communist Party meetings?

MR. BURROWS. Meetings at which Communists were present. *Silence.* Those were bad years for me. In personal trouble. My mother and father both died. I had to seek help from a psychiatrist. That whole period is kind of a painful, very painful period to me. *Silence.*

THE CHAIRMAN. They were *Communist Party* meetings?

MR. BURROWS. I imagine they could be called Communist Party meetings. I imagine so. I really am vague on that. I am sorry if I sound over-vague. . . .

Abe Burrows's testimony did sound over-vague to Paramount. They dropped their option on *Guys and Dolls* at once. The film was finally made by another company only when Burrows's case had been appealed to the unofficial chief justice of the United States in those years, the columnist George E. Sokolsky.

Elia Kazan (*Wide World Photos*).

Elia Kazan came before a subcommittee of HUAC, in closed session, April 10, 1952.

MR. KAZAN, *reading.* I was a member of the Communist Party from '34 until '36. For the 19 months of my membership, I was assigned to a "unit" composed of members of the Group Theater company. These were: Lewis Leverett, co-leader of the unit; J. Edward Bromberg, co-leader of the unit, deceased; Phoebe Brand, later Mrs. Morris Carnovsky, I was instrumental in bringing her into the Party; Morris Carnovsky; Paula Miller, later Mrs. Lee Strasberg; Clifford Odets; Art Smith; Tony Kraber, he recruited me into the Party. . . . I have placed a copy of this affidavit with Spyros P. Skouras, President of 20th Century-Fox.

THE INVESTIGATOR. Mr. Kazan, it is only through the assistance of people such as you that we have been able to bring the attention of the American people to the Communist conspiracy for world domination.

Tony Kraber was summoned before the Committee three years later accompanied by his attorney Leonard B. Boudin.

INVESTIGATOR. Mr. Kraber, were you a member of a Communist Party organization within the Group Theater in 1934 or '35?

MR. KRABER. I believe this question to be an invasion of my rights, and I decline to answer on the ground of the First Amendment and the Fifth Amendment.

INVESTIGATOR. Mr. Elia Kazan testified that he was recruited into a Communist Party organization within the Group Theater by Tony Kraber.

Tony Kraber and Leonard B. Boudin (*UPI*).

MR. KRABER. Is this the Kazan that signed the contract for $500,000 the day after he gave names to this Committee?

INVESTIGATOR. Would it change the facts if he did?

MR. KRABER. Would you sell your brothers for $500,000?

CM 1. Do you say that Mr. Kazan committed perjury before this Committee?

MR. KRABER. I will decline to answer this question.

INVESTIGATOR. Did you recruit Mr. Kazan into the Communist Party?

MR. KRABER. I decline to answer on the ground of the First Amendment and the Fifth Amendment.

On May 5, 1953 Jerome Robbins came before the Committee in the U.S. Court House, Foley Square, Manhattan.

THE CHAIRMAN. I understand you desire the lights be turned off, Mr. Robbins?

MR. ROBBINS. Yes.

INVESTIGATOR. You were at one time a member of the Communist Party, is that correct?

MR. ROBBINS. Yes.

INVESTIGATOR. For how long were you a member?

MR. ROBBINS. I attended my first meeting in the spring of '44. At one of the earliest meetings, I was asked in what way did dialectical materialism help me to do my ballet *Fancy Free!*
Laughter.

INVESTIGATOR. Will you tell the Committee what brought about the termination of your relationship with the Communist Party?

MR. ROBBINS. The last meeting I attended was in '47. A fight broke out. Everyone began arguing and yelling. I suddenly realized I was in the midst of chaos, of an unorganized frantic group. It was too much. I didn't know what I was doing here. I had no interest in continuing.
Pause.

INVESTIGATOR. Who recruited you into the Party, Mr. Robbins?

MR. ROBBINS. Miss Lettie Stever.

INVESTIGATOR. Will you give us the names of other persons in this group?

MR. ROBBINS. Lloyd Gough. Lionel Berman.

INVESTIGATOR. A Party member asked you to what extent

Jerome Robbins (*UPI*).

dialectical materialism influenced you in the production of *Fancy Free?*

MR. ROBBINS. Yes.

INVESTIGATOR. Who *was* that?

MR. ROBBINS. Madeline Lee.

INVESTIGATOR. Can you recall the names of other persons?

MR. ROBBINS. Elliott Sullivan.

INVESTIGATOR. Elliott Sullivan. Do you know how Elliott Sullivan was employed?

MR. ROBBINS. I believe he was an actor. *Pause.* Edna Ocko.

INVESTIGATOR. How can you identify her as a member? Is there any particular incident?

MR. ROBBINS. Yes. She was in the middle of this argument at the last meeting.

INVESTIGATOR. All right.

MR. ROBBINS. Jerome Chodorov.

INVESTIGATOR. Jerome Chodorov.

MR. ROBBINS. And Edward Chodorov.

INVESTIGATOR. Edward Chodorov.

CM 1. Mr. Robbins, I want to compliment you on what you have done! We have had men before us who have referred to people who have named others as "stool pigeons," "informers." You realize, no doubt, that when you volunteered the names of Communists you would be put in that class?

MR. ROBBINS. Yes, sir.

CM 1. You did it with your eyes open?

MR. ROBBINS. I did it according to my conscience.

CM 1. Now, I have a very personal question—and I have never met you, I have never talked with you before, have I?

MR. ROBBINS. No, sir.

CM 1. What is it in your conscience that makes *you*, certainly one of the top men in your profession, one who has reached the *pinnacle* in your art, willing to come here and testify as you have today, in spite of the fact that you knew some people would put you down as a "stool pigeon"?

MR. ROBBINS. I've examined myself. I think I made a great mistake in entering the Communist Party. I feel I am now doing the right thing as an American.

CM 1. Again, I want to compliment you! You are in a wonderful place, through your art, your music, your talent which God blessed you with, to be vigorous and positive in promoting Americanism in contrast to Communism! Let me suggest that you use that great talent which God has blessed you with to put into ballets in some way, to put into music in some way, that interpretation!

MR. ROBBINS. Sir, all my works have been acclaimed for their American quality particularly.

CM 1. But let me urge you to put even more of that in it!

THE CHAIRMAN. Mr. Robbins, you have performed a patriotic service to the Committee. Congress and the American people are very thankful to you.

Elliott Sullivan and Bella Abzug (*UPI*).

Elliott Sullivan was summoned before the Committee two years later accompanied by his attorney Bella Abzug.

INVESTIGATOR. Mr. Martin Berkeley described a fraction meeting of the Communist Party which he said Elliott Sullivan attended. Mr. Sullivan, are you acquainted with Martin Berkeley?

MR. SULLIVAN. This committee does not have the right to ask me about my associations. As for the long, tired list of men who have sold their honor and dignity for a mess of pottage, for a job, for a movie contract, I believe they will be judged by the decent people in this country.

INVESTIGATOR. Are you acquainted with Jerome Robbins?

MR. SULLIVAN. I know him. I used to know him. I will amend that definitely: I used to know him.

INVESTIGATOR. When did you cease to know him? When he testified before this Committee?

MR. SULLIVAN. Will you repeat the question?

INVESTIGATOR. I am asking whether the time you ceased to know Jerome Robbins began when he testified before this Committee?

MR. SULLIVAN. I would say that is the case. Yes.

Martin Berkeley was a screenwriter who, after initial hesitation, had come in to the Committee and named one hundred and sixty-two names.

MR. BERKELEY. My name was mentioned by cooperative witness Richard Collins, and I sent a very silly telegram to the Committee. I charged Mr. Collins with perjury and said I had never been a member of the Communist Party, which was not true. I did it in a moment of panic and was a damn fool.

Elliott Sullivan (*UPI*).

INVESTIGATOR. Since that time you have determined that you will aid this Committee in every possible way?

MR. BERKELEY. Yes, sir.

INVESTIGATOR. Tell the Committee what the Communist Party was attempting to accomplish and the methods by which they expected to accomplish it.

MR. BERKELEY. I am reminded of one day at Lionel Stander's house. He came in all excited. He says, "By golly, I got away with it." I said, "What did you get away with?" because—I don't want to refer to him again as a screwball, but the man was a screwball! He said, "Well, I was shooting this picture, and I had to wait for the elevator, and I pressed the button and there was a pause, and the director said, 'Whistle something and fill in,' so I whistled four bars of the Internationale." That was about the extent of what the Communists were able to do!

INVESTIGATOR. Tell the Committee when and where the Hollywood section of the Communist Party was organized.

MR. BERKELEY. By a strange coincidence, in my house. In June 1937. In my house out on Beverly Glen. We were honored by the presence of many functionaries. The spirit was swell.

CM 1. Is that "swell" or "smell"?

MR. BERKELEY. "Smell" I would say now!

INVESTIGATOR. Give us the names of those in attendance who were members of the Communist Party.

MR. BERKELEY. Well, in addition to those I've mentioned, there was Donald Ogden Stewart, Dorothy Parker, her husband Allen Campbell, my old friend Dashiell Hammett, now in jail in New York for his activities, and that excellent playwright Lillian Hellman.

Martin Berkeley (*Acme Photo*).

Lillian Hellman (*Graphic House*).

Summoned to Washington in May 1952 to answer Martin Berkeley's charges, Lillian Hellman wrote a letter to the Chairman.

Dear Mr. Wood,

I have been advised by counsel that I have a constitutional privilege to decline to answer any questions about my political opinions, activities, and associations, on the grounds of self-incrimination. I do not wish to claim this privilege. I have nothing to hide from your Committee and there is nothing in my life of which I am ashamed. I am willing to testify before the representatives of our Government as to my own opinions and actions, regardless of any risks to myself. But I am advised by counsel that if I answer questions about myself, I will have waived my rights under the Fifth Amendment and could be forced legally to answer questions about others. If I refuse to do so, I can be cited for contempt. This is very difficult for a layman to understand. But there is one principle that I do understand: I am not willing, now or in the future, to bring bad trouble to people who, in my past association with them, were completely innocent of any talk or any action that was disloyal or subversive. I do not like subversion or disloyalty in any form, and if I had ever seen any, I would have considered it my duty to have reported it to the proper authorities. But to hurt innocent people whom I knew many years ago in order to save myself is, to me, inhuman and indecent and dishonorable. I cannot and will not cut my conscience to fit this year's fashions, even though I long ago came to the conclusion that I was not a political person and could have no comfortable place in any political group. I was raised in an old-fashioned American tradition and there were certain homely things that were taught to me: to try to tell the truth, not to bear false witness, not to harm my neighbor, to be loyal to my country. I respected these ideals of Christian honor and did as well with them as I knew how. It is my belief that you will agree with these simple rules of human decency and not expect me to violate the good American tradition from which they spring. I am prepared to waive the privilege against self-incrimination and tell you everything you wish to know about my views or actions if your committee will refrain from asking me to name other people.

Sincerely yours,
Lillian Hellman.

The Chairman informed Miss Hellman that the Committee could "not be placed in the attitude of trading with the witnesses as to what they will testify to." Miss Hellman invoked the Fifth Amendment.

Almost as informative as the screenwriter Martin Berkeley was the actor Marc Lawrence.

INVESTIGATOR. How long did you remain a member of the Communist Party, Mr. Lawrence?

MR. LAWRENCE. I didn't believe myself to be a *member,* in terms of participation. I merely investigated and wanted to hear what these people had to say. About 1946 I did one play for the Actors' Lab—

INVESTIGATOR. What was the title of the play?

MR. LAWRENCE. The title of the play was *Volpone.*

INVESTIGATOR. Your primary interest was to investigate. What do you mean by that?

MR. LAWRENCE. Well, I am a curious kind of schmoe. I am the kind of a guy that listens to speeches. The guy comes over to me and says, "Listen, that sounds pretty

Marc Lawrence (*Acme Photo*).

good, why don't you defend this idea?" I got involved that way. I didn't defend the idea, I listened to the idea, I investigated the idea. I am not interested in the idea. It is a very destructive thing. It has been to me. Having been a member of the Communist Party has been a great error in my life. I have never voted the Communist ticket, I have been a registered Democrat. The Communist Party is very destructive. I will not, as a patriot, defend any of its interests. I feel that strongly about it! I will defend this country in case of war with Russia, I will defend it with my life!

INVESTIGATOR. Give us the names of those who were members with you in this cell within the Actors' Lab.

MR. LAWRENCE. J. Edward Bromberg, Karen Morley, Morris Carnovsky. . . .

INVESTIGATOR. You stated Lionel Stander was the one who introduced you into the Communist Party.

MR. LAWRENCE. He said to me, "Get to know this stuff and you will make out more with the dames!" This is the guy, this is the introduction!

On May 6, 1953 Lionel Stander, accompanied by his attorney Leonard B. Boudin, came before the Committee at his own request to deal with the charges of Marc Lawrence and Martin Berkeley.

MR. STANDER. Mr. Velde, I would like it very much if you turned off the lights and discontinued the television cameras, as I am a professional performer and I only appear on TV for entertainment or for philanthropic organizations, and I consider this a matter that doesn't fall into either category.

THE CHAIRMAN. You mean a man who has been before the cameras would have difficulty testifying?

MR. STANDER. Yes. When I am before a camera I am an entertainer, not a witness.

THE CHAIRMAN. You are before the United States Government now!

MR. STANDER. Which is a very serious thing, sir.

THE CHAIRMAN. A very serious thing.

MR. STANDER. If I were here as an entertainer, I wouldn't have any objection, but—

THE CHAIRMAN. The Committee desires to give the public the information that comes before it in all shapes and forms, and the *excuse* that you are an entertainer—

MR. STANDER. That isn't an *excuse*, it is a fact.

THE CHAIRMAN. —has no bearing whatsoever.

MR. STANDER. I resent the fact that you say it is an excuse. I *am* an entertainer, and it is quite different to come before the camera in a carefully rehearsed script and, on the other hand, to come before the camera as a witness before a Committee.

THE CHAIRMAN. Now, Mr. Stander—

MR. STANDER. I would appreciate it if you would turn the lights and cameras off.

Lionel Stander and Leonard B. Boudin (*UPI*).

MR. BOUDIN. It's been done for other witnesses!

THE CHAIRMAN. Because it would make them nervous and/or interfere with the testimony they had to give.

MR. STANDER. I am not exactly calm this morning. I am playing in another city, and haven't had any sleep. I was unable to get a room in a hotel.

THE CHAIRMAN. Well, Mr. Stander, let me ask you—

MR. STANDER. I've been in Philadelphia, and—

THE CHAIRMAN. If we do turn off the cameras, will you answer the questions put to you by counsel?

MR. STANDER. I intend to cooperate! I took an oath, and I believe in my oaths!

THE CHAIRMAN. In that case, will the television and newsreel cameras please desist, and will the still photographers take their pictures and kindly retire during the witness's testimony?

Pause while this happens.

INVESTIGATOR. The witness appeared before this Committee in 1940, denied having been a member of the Communist Party, and stated that he never intended to be. In 1951 Marc Lawrence testified before the Committee and alluded to this witness. On the following day a telegram was received in which the witness denied the statements made by Mr. Lawrence and requested an opportunity to appear before the Committee.

THE CHAIRMAN. This matter has been before the Committee for two years?

INVESTIGATOR. Yes.

MR. STANDER. I tried to get an *immediate* hearing! I sent a letter to every member of the Committee! I went in person to Washington and saw Congressman Kearney, who assured me—

CM 1. Mr. Stander—

MR. STANDER. —I would have an immediate hearing. It was

important. Merely receiving the subpoena caused me to be blacklisted in radio, television, and motion pictures. At the same time I sued the witness who perjured himself before this Committee, Mr. Marc Lawrence, in the State Supreme Court of New York, which ruled that he enjoyed Congressional immunity. However, if he—

THE CHAIRMAN. Mr. Stander, we are not interested in extraneous matters.

MR. STANDER. Extraneous? When a man comes directly from the psychopathic ward! I informed the Committeemen that this psychopath was used as a witness against me and, under advice of counsel, fled to Europe and is still a refugee from this court case.

CM 2. Do I understand, Mr. Stander, you are here to answer the sixty-four-dollar question?

MR. STANDER. I will answer *every* question! I have made an oath, and I'm not in the habit of violating my word, even when I *don't* swear an oath.

INVESTIGATOR. Mr. Stander, will you tell the Committee, please, when and where were you born?

MR. STANDER. New York City, January 11, 1908.

INVESTIGATOR. What is your occupation?

MR. STANDER. I'm basically an actor. I've been a newspaper reporter, I've been a director of stage entertainments for the Red Cross, the Air Force, the Kiwanis, junior and senior chambers of commerce, Elks, Moose, and other organizations with animal names. I've produced two Broadway plays. I've been a theatrical person for the last twenty-six years. With an occasional venture into journalism.

INVESTIGATOR. Have you also done screen writing or acting?

MR. STANDER. I've done screen acting. I've written a script or two for the screen.

Lionel Stander (*UPI*).

INVESTIGATOR. How long were you a screen actor, and where?

MR. STANDER. Well, my first jobs were in the old silent days as a kid actor. I worked with Marian Davies at the old Hearst Cosmopolitan.

INVESTIGATOR. How long did you remain in Hollywood?

MR. STANDER. Until I exposed the criminal records of Browne and Bioff, the racketeer-gangster officials who later went to jail. Because I exposed them one week before Westbrook Pegler exposed them in the paper, I was blacklisted by the Motion Picture Producers Association!

INVESTIGATOR. How long did you continue as an actor?

MR. STANDER. After the major studios blacklisted me, I worked for independent producers—

INVESTIGATOR. Approximately—

MR. STANDER. —up until Marc Lawrence mentioned my name, or rather, until Larry Parks said he didn't know me as a Communist.

INVESTIGATOR. Let me—

MR. STANDER. That appeared in the paper. Just to have my name appear in association with this Committee! It's like the Spanish Inquisition!

INVESTIGATOR. Let me remind you—

MR. STANDER. You may not be burned but you can't help coming away a little singed.

INVESTIGATOR. How long did you engage in screen acting?

MR. STANDER. '35 to '48 or '9, except for a period in the Air Force. *He looks at a paper.* And while I'm looking at it here I notice the Chief of Staff gave me letters and autographed pictures attesting to my excellent service record and character!

INVESTIGATOR. What is the date of—

MR. STANDER. I see a citation from the Red Cross, the war bond drive, the treasury department, and here's a tribute from the Armed Forces Radio Service, "Dear Mr. Stander, may I extend my appreciation for your splendid. . . ."

THE CHAIRMAN. Mr. Stander, if there is some part of your career you are proud of—

MR. STANDER. I am proud of *everything!*

THE CHAIRMAN. You have made some self-serving statements, and—

MR. STANDER. Does the Committee charge me with being a Communist?

THE CHAIRMAN. Mr. Stander, will you let me tell you? Will you be quiet while I tell you what you are here for?

MR. STANDER. Yes, I'd like to hear!

THE CHAIRMAN. You are here to give us information which will enable us to do the work assigned to us by the House of Representatives: to investigate reports regarding subversive activies in the United States.

MR. STANDER. Well, I am more than willing to cooperate—

THE CHAIRMAN. Now, just a minute.

MR. STANDER. —because I know of subversive activities in in the entertainment industry and elsewhere!

THE CHAIRMAN. Mr. Stander, the Committee is interested—

MR. STANDER. If you're *interested,* I can tell you right now.

THE CHAIRMAN. —primarily in any subversive knowledge you have—

MR. STANDER. I have *knowledge* of subversive action! I know of a group of fanatics who are trying to undermine the Constitution of the United States by depriving artists of life, liberty, and pursuit of happiness without due process of law! I can cite instances! I can tell names. I am one of the first victims, if you are interested. A group of ex-Bundists, America Firsters, and anti-Semites, people who hate everybody, Negroes, minority groups, and most likely themselves—

THE CHAIRMAN. Now, Mr. Stander, unless you begin to answer these questions and act like a witness in a reasonable, dignified manner, under the rules of the Committee, I will be forced to have you removed from this room!

Pause.

MR. STANDER. I am deeply shocked, Mr. Chairman!

CM 2. Mr. Stander, let me—

MR. STANDER. I don't mean to be contemptuous of this committee at all!

THE CHAIRMAN. Will you—

MR. STANDER. I want to cooperate with your attempt to unearth subversive activities. I began to tell you about them, and I'm shocked by your cutting me off. I am not a dupe, or a dope, or a moe, or a schmoe, and I'm not ashamed of anything I said in public or private!

INVESTIGATOR. Mr. Stander, is it correct to say you were an actor in Hollywood between '35 and '48 with the exception of your period in the armed services, '42 to '44?

MR. STANDER. Yes, sir.

INVESTIGATOR. What were some of your screen credits?

MR. STANDER. I made about a hundred screenplays. Luckily I've forgotten most of them.

INVESTIGATOR. Give us a few of the major ones.

MR. STANDER. Well, *Deeds Goes to Town, Specter of the Rose, A Star Is Born.* . . .

INVESTIGATOR. Do you recall whether you left Hollywood in '48 or in '49?

MR. STANDER. I'm not sure. I made a tour of the night-club circuit, which was the only thing left to me after being blacklisted by the major studios—

INVESTIGATOR. Will you tell—

MR. STANDER. —by merely newspaper accusation, without anybody charging me with anything. In fact, the last time I appeared here the Chairman *said* this Committee didn't charge me with anything, and I swore under oath—I would like, if you want, to introduce the record of my testimony here in August 27, 1940.

THE CHAIRMAN. Well, you are not charged with anything.

MR. STANDER. I am not charged with lying under oath? You are not charging me with being a Communist?

CM 2. Will you subside until the Chairman finishes?

THE CHAIRMAN. You are brought here as a witness.

MR. STANDER. I am a witness—

THE CHAIRMAN. Please don't—

MR. STANDER. —not a defendant. I haven't been accused of anything! I want that very straight, because through newspaper headlines people get peculiar attitudes. Mere appearance here is tantamount to being blacklisted, because people say, "What is an actor doing in front of the Un-American Activities Committee?"

CM 2. Why did you want to appear before the Committee so badly, then?

MR. STANDER. Because I was told by my agent, if the Committee allowed me to refute Marc Lawrence's testimony, I'd be able to get back in motion pictures. One of the biggest TV agencies told my agent that, if I could again swear I wasn't a Communist, I'd have my own TV program! Which meant one hundred fifty thousand dollars a year to me.

CM 2. Mr. Stander—

MR. STANDER. So I had a hundred-and-fifty-thousand-buck motive—

CM 2. Mr. Stander, will you subside?

MR. STANDER. —for coming before the Committee!

CM 2. If you will just subside and answer the questions—

MR. STANDER. Are you inferring—

CM 2. Now, just a minute, Mr. Stander.

MR. STANDER. —anything I said wasn't the truth?

CM 2. Unless you do that, your performance is not going to be regarded as funny.

MR. STANDER. I want to state right now I was not—

CM 2. Will you please subside?

MR. STANDER. —trying to be funny.

CM 2. If you continue, I am going to ask the Chairman to turn on the cameras so your performance may be recorded for posterity!

MR. STANDER. Mr. Chairman, may I state, first, that I have never been more deadly serious in my life.

CM 2. All right, then—

MR. STANDER. If anything I said seemed humorous, I assure you it doesn't mirror what I feel. My entire career and the respect of my fellow artists and the American people is at stake. I don't think that is very funny.

CM 2. I am a new member of this Committee, and I want you to say what you have to say. But in the proper way.

INVESTIGATOR. Mr. Stander, tell the Committee what your educational training has consisted of.

MR. STANDER. Public schools in New York, various prep schools, a few colleges, the University of North Carolina. . . .

INVESTIGATOR. Now, Mr. Stander, the investigation the Committee has made would indicate that you have special knowledge of things that the Committee is inquiring about. Marc Lawrence testified he attended meetings of the Party, quote, "in different homes in Hollywood. Lester Cole was there, and the guy who introduced me to the Communist Party, Lionel Stander," unquote. Harold J. Ashe was asked the

125

Lionel Stander (*UPI*).

names of professional units whose membership was kept secret. Here is his testimony: "Lucy Stander, the wife of J. Stander, also known as Lionel Stander—"

MR. STANDER. I'm not married.

INVESTIGATOR. Or your former wife.

MR. STANDER. Which one?

INVESTIGATOR. Well, the name mentioned here was Lucy.

CM 1. Do you remember that name?

MR. STANDER. Yeah, I remember her. Vaguely.

INVESTIGATOR. Let me read that again: "Lucy Stander, at that time the wife of J. Stander, also known as Lionel Stander—"

MR. STANDER. What year was that?

INVESTIGATOR. Along about '36.

MR. STANDER. I wasn't married to Lucy in '36.

CM 4. It was evidently the time you *were* married to Lucy. You would know when you were married to Lucy, wouldn't you?

MR. STANDER. Yes. We were separated in '35.

INVESTIGATOR, *reading.* "Lionel Stander was definitely a member of this group." Then, the testimony of Mr. Martin Berkeley: "I met Lionel Stander who later became chairman of the actors' fraction. He called me over into a corner and introduced me to Comrade Harry Bridges." So, I want to ask you whether you were a member of the Communist Party at any time between 1935 and 1948?

MR. STANDER. I made a statement under oath to this Committee in 1940. I'd like you to read it into the record. You've asked me a question that took about twenty minutes. This will take exactly three minutes.

INVESTIGATOR. Will you answer my question?

MR. STANDER. I swore in 1940 that I was not a member of the Communist Party. I also—

INVESTIGATOR. What do you say now?

MR. STANDER. I also swore in 1940, before the Los Angeles grand jury and its district attorney, and I forced my way in there, I was a voluntary witness, and one of the witnesses used here, John Leech, who was later characterized by Judge Landis as a psychopathic liar, made statements similar to the statements made by Marc Lawrence and others. I swore under oath, and the district attorney's bureau saw fit to clear me! And the grand jury said I was a fine, patriotic, American citizen! I am reading from my 1940 testimony—

THE CHAIRMAN. Now, Mr. Stander—

MR. STANDER. —which is the first time it ever has been released to the press—

THE CHAIRMAN. —you promised me you would answer the question!

MR. STANDER. I have also sworn under oath in an affidavit for the Royal Canadian Air Force and the United States Air Force. . . . I worked in a very sensitive spot in the headquarters' staff, and it's standard operating procedure to be cleared by the FBI. I can't see it would serve the purposes of this Committee to ask me about 1934, '35, '36—

THE CHAIRMAN. Mr. Stander—

MR. STANDER. And, incidentally, while you're mentioning that, there are contradictions.

THE CHAIRMAN. Mr. Stander, will you—

MR. STANDER. Mrs. Ashe said she collected dues from me in '34—

THE CHAIRMAN. Mr. Stander—

MR. STANDER. I wasn't in Hollywood then! Her own husband said it was in '36!

THE CHAIRMAN. Mr. Stander—

MR. STANDER. And my wife left me in '35.

THE CHAIRMAN. Mr. Stander, may I remind you that you have promised to answer the question—

MR. STANDER. I have answered.

THE CHAIRMAN. —and now will you—

MR. STANDER. If any of these charges are true, why haven't I been indicted?

THE CHAIRMAN. Will you now answer the question—

MR. STANDER. I was asked a twenty-five-minute question and I can't even give a two-minute answer. I don't think that is fair!

CM 2. Mr. Stander, you have been asked a straightforward question: whether or not you were a Communist during a certain period. Now, answer that—

MR. STANDER. I swore under oath—

CM 2. —yes or no—

MR. STANDER. I swore—

CM 2. —or refuse to answer it on constitutional grounds.

MR. STANDER. I swore under oath in 1940, and that was covered by this same Committee.

CM 4. Why don't you swear under oath now?

MR. STANDER. You want me to give you the reason?

CM 4. Yes.

MR. STANDER. Because by using psychopaths—and I have the letter here giving the mental history of Marc Lawrence, who came from a mental sanitorium—he suffered a mental breakdown, and you used that psychopath and this man Leech, who the district attorney and the grand jury didn't believe, and they cleared me —so, I don't want to be responsible for a whole stable of informers, stool pigeons, psychopaths, and ex-political heretics, who come in here beating their breasts and saying "I'm awfully sorry, I didn't know what I was doing, please, I want *absolution,* get me back into pictures!" They will do anything *to get back into pictures!* They will mention names! They will name *anybody!*

INVESTIGATOR. Are you acquainted with Martin Berkeley?

MR. STANDER. Any question by stool pigeons, informers, psychopathic liars—for instance, Mr. Berkeley— First, he said he wasn't a member of the Communist Party, then, when he realized you had the goods on him, he came here and rattled off one hundred fifty names. This is an *incredible* witness!

THE CHAIRMAN. Do you decline to answer that question?

MR. STANDER. I resent the inference that anyone who invokes the Fifth, which our forefathers fought for, is guilty of anything. My name is Stander. The name was adopted because in feudal Spain my ancestors didn't have the protection of the United States Constitution and were religious refugees. And you know that the Puritans, the people that established this country, used this right. I have done a little research since you called me. The first instance was—

INVESTIGATOR. Will you answer the question I asked you?

MR. STANDER. —and I am not being sacrilegious—when Jesus Christ was asked by Pontius Pilate, "These judges have a lot of witnesses against you?" And he said nothing. *Pause.*

THE CHAIRMAN. Now will you answer the question? *Pause.*

MR. STANDER, *quietly.* I decline under the First Amendment, which entitles me to freedom of belief, under the Fifth Amendment—in which there is no inference of guilt— and under the Ninth Amendment, which gives me the right to get up in the union hall, which I did, and introduce a resolution condemning this Committee for its abuse of powers in attempting to impose censorship upon the American theater.

INVESTIGATOR. Now, Mr. Stander—

MR. STANDER, *still quiet*. And, finally, I can't understand why a question dating back to 1935 concerning statements made by a bunch of stool pigeons and informers can aid this Committee in recommending legislation to Congress. The question is not relevant to the purposes of this Committee.

Lionel Stander remained on the blacklist.

Zero Mostel, October 14, 1955.

INVESTIGATOR. I have now before me a photostatic copy of a flier advertising a public meeting under the auspices of *Mainstream* magazine. The flier is entitled "Artists Fight Back Against Un-American Thought Control." The speakers include Zero Mostel. Mr. Mostel, were you a speaker on that occasion?

MR. MOSTEL. I decline to answer on constitutional grounds.

CM 1. According to your own testimony, you were not a member of the Communist Party when you came into this room. I cannot help but feel, Witness, that there was a time when you *were* a member of the Communist Party.

MR. MOSTEL. That is a feeling, not knowledge.

MR. MOSTEL'S ATTORNEY, *loudly.* You must be aware of Harvey Matusow and others like him who admitted that they falsely charged membership!

CM 1, *loudly.* Harvey Matusow is not before this Committee!

CM 2. Order, gentlemen!

MR. MOSTEL. Don't fight, boys!
Pause.

CM 2. May I say I can think of no greater way to parade one's political beliefs than to appear under the auspices of a Communist publication on the same platform with Dalton Trumbo, Hanns Eisler, Dorothy Parker, Howard Fast, and Zero Mostel.

MR. MOSTEL. I do want to say. . . . Maybe it is impolitic for me to say this. *Pause. If* I appeared there, what if I did a butterfly at rest? There is no crime in making anybody laugh.

CM 2. If your interpretation of a butterfly at rest brought any money into the coffers of the Communist Party you

Zero Mostel (*Wide World Photos*).

contributed directly to the propaganda effort of the Communist Party.

MR. MOSTEL. Suppose I had the *urge* to do the butterfly at rest somewhere?

CM 1. Yes, but please, when you have the urge, don't have such an urge to put the butterfly at rest by putting some money in the Communist Party coffers as a result of that urge to put the butterfly to rest.

Zero Mostel remained on the blacklist.

Arthur Miller, May 21, 1956.

INVESTIGATOR. In 1953 did you criticize Elia Kazan as a renegade intellectual?

MR. MILLER. No.

INVESTIGATOR. As an informer?

MR. MILLER. No.

INVESTIGATOR. After Kazan had been your producer, worked with you in your plays, and came down to Washington and testified before a Committee, Yes, I have been a Communist, yes, I identify so-and-so and so-and-so as people who were in the conspiracy with me, did you break with him?

MR. MILLER. I broke with him—though that word is not descriptive of my act. There are private reasons involved which I don't believe are of interest here.

Pause.

INVESTIGATOR. Tell us about these meetings with Communist writers which you said you attended in New York City. Who invited you there?

MR. MILLER. I don't know.

INVESTIGATOR. Who was there when you walked into the room?

Pause.

MR. MILLER. I understand the philosophy behind this question and I want you to understand mine. I am trying to—and I will—protect my sense of myself. I could not use the name of another person and bring trouble on him. I ask you not to ask me that question.

CM 1. We do not accept your reasons for refusing to answer. If you do not answer, you are placing yourself in contempt.

INVESTIGATOR. Was Arnaud d'Usseau chairman at this meet-

Arthur Miller (*Wide World Photos*).

ing of Communist writers in 1947 at which you were
in attendance?
Pause.

MR. MILLER. All I can say, sir, is that my conscience will not
permit me to use the name of another person.

**By 373 votes to nine the House of Representatives found
Arthur Miller in contempt of Congress.**

Paul Robeson, 1956. During the early fifties, an attempt was made by the Government and the press to wipe Paul Robeson off the record. On at least one occasion, willingness to denounce Robeson was made the test of a movie star's patriotism, the movie star being Robeson's old friend José Ferrer. Otherwise Ferrer's new movie, *Moulin Rouge*, would be picketed and shut down by friends of HUAC. Director Willand of the American Legion stated:

The American Legion expresses disapproval of the distribution of *Moulin Rouge* until such time as the personnel connected with it evidence sincere cooperation with their government. The Legion disapproves of the distribution of the picture because of the various front records of José Ferrer and John Huston.

Whereupon, the *Hollywood Reporter* announced:

JOSÉ FERRER BLASTS SOVIET PEACE PRIZE. "I condemn Paul Robeson's acceptance of Stalin's so-called Peace Prize," Ferrer said as he lambasted Robeson.

The columnist George Sokolsky summed up:

No one has ever denounced Paul Robeson with such accurate pinpointing of his unforgivable sins against his native land as José Ferrer.

The Legion's opposition to *Moulin Rouge* was then withdrawn. What HUAC saw as its contribution to the war against Robeson was to help the State Department keep the singer from travelling abroad. Robeson commented:

I am not in any conspiracy. It should be plain to everybody and especially to Negroes that, if the Government had evidence to back up that charge, they would have tried to put me *under* their jail. They have no such evidence. In 1946, at a hearing in California, I testified under oath that I was not a member of the Communist Party. Since then I have refused to give testimony to that fact. There is no mystery in this. I have made it a matter of principle to refuse to comply with any demand that infringes upon the Constitutional rights of all Americans.

INVESTIGATOR. Paul Robeson, will you please come forward? Identify yourself by name, residence and occupation.

MR. ROBESON. My name is Paul Robeson. I live at 16 Jumel Terrace, New York City. I am an actor and singer by occupation, and law on the side now and then.

INVESTIGATOR. Are you appearing today in response to a subpoena served upon you by the House Committee on Un-American Activities?

MR. ROBESON. Do I have the privilege of asking whom I am addressing and who is addressing me?

INVESTIGATOR. I am Richard Arens.

MR. ROBESON. What is your position?

INVESTIGATOR. I am Director of the Staff. The subpoena commands you to produce certain documents, including all the United States passports issued to you for travel outside the continental limits of the United States. Do you have those documents?

MR. ROBESON. No. I have moved several times in the last year, and we have got a lot of stuff still packed. If they are unpacked I will be glad to send them to you.

INVESTIGATOR. Did you file a passport application on July 2, 1954?

MR. ROBESON. I have filed about twenty-five in the last few months.

Paul Robeson (*Wide World Photos*).

Richard Arens (*Wide World Photos*).

INVESTIGATOR. In July of 1954, were you requested to submit a non-Communist affidavit?

MR. ROBESON. Under no conditions would I think of signing any such affidavit. It is a contradiction of the rights of American citizens.

INVESTIGATOR. Are you now a member of the Communist Party?

MR. ROBESON. Oh please, please, please.

CM 1. Please answer, will you, Mr. Robeson?

MR. ROBESON. What *is* the Communist Party? What do you mean by that?

CM 1, *to the chairman.* I ask that you direct the witness to answer the question.

MR. ROBESON. What do you mean by the Communist Party? As far as I know it is a legal party like the Republican Party and the Democratic Party. Do you mean a party of people who have sacrificed for my people, and for all Americans and workers, that they can live in dignity? Do you mean *that* party?

INVESTIGATOR. Are you now a member of the Communist Party?

MR. ROBESON. Would you like to come to the ballot box when I vote and take out the ballot and see?

INVESTIGATOR. Mr. Chairman, I respectfully suggest that the witness be directed to answer that question.

THE CHAIRMAN. You are directed to answer the question.

MR. ROBESON. I invoke the Fifth Amendment.

INVESTIGATOR. Do you honestly apprehend that if you told this Committee truthfully—

MR. ROBESON. I have no desire to consider anything, and it is none of your business what I would like to do. I invoke the Fifth Amendment. And forget it.

THE CHAIRMAN. You are directed to answer that question.

MR. ROBESON. I invoke the Fifth Amendment, and so I am answering it, am I not?

INVESTIGATOR. I respectfully suggest the witness be ordered to answer the question whether, if he gave us a truthful answer, he would be supplying information which might be used against him in a criminal proceeding.

THE CHAIRMAN. You are directed to answer, Mr. Robeson.

MR. ROBESON. Gentlemen, in the first place, wherever I have been in the world, the first to die in the struggle against Fascism were the Communists. I laid many wreaths upon the graves of Communists. *Pause.* It is not criminal. The Fifth Amendment does not infer criminality. Chief Justice Warren has been very clear on that. I invoke the Fifth Amendment.

INVESTIGATOR. Have you ever been known under the name of "John Thomas"?

MR. ROBESON. Oh, please, does somebody here want—are you suggesting—do you want me to put up for perjury some place? "John Thomas"! My name is Paul Robeson, and anything I have to say I have said in public all over the world. That is why I am here today.

CM 1, *to the chairman.* I ask that you direct the witness to answer the question. He is making a speech.

MR. ROBESON'S ATTORNEY. Excuse me, Mr. Arens, may we have the photographers take their pictures, and then desist? It is rather nerve-racking for them to be there.

THE CHAIRMAN. They will take the pictures.

MR. ROBESON. I am used to it and I have been in moving pictures. Do you want me to pose for it good? Do you want me to smile? *Indicating the Investigator,* I can't smile when I'm talking to *him.*

INVESTIGATOR. I ask you to affirm or deny the fact that your Communist Party name was "John Thomas."

143

MR. ROBESON. I invoke the Fifth Amendment. This is really ridiculous.

INVESTIGATOR. Now, tell this Committee whether or not you know Nathan Gregory Silvermaster.

Mr. Robeson laughs.

CM 1. Mr. Chairman, this is not a laughing matter.

MR. ROBESON. It *is* a laughing matter! This is complete nonsense!

INVESTIGATOR. Have you ever known Nathan Gregory Silvermaster?

MR. ROBESON. I invoke the Fifth Amendment.

INVESTIGATOR. Do you honestly apprehend that if you told whether you know Nathan Gregory Silvermaster you would be supplying information that could be used against you in a criminal proceeding?

MR. ROBESON. I have not the slightest idea what you are talking about. I invoke the Fifth—

INVESTIGATOR. I suggest, Mr. Chairman, that the witness be directed to answer that question.

THE CHAIRMAN. You are directed to answer the question.

MR. ROBESON. I invoke the Fifth.

CM 1. The witness talks very loud when he makes a speech, but when he invokes the Fifth Amendment I can't hear him.

MR. ROBESON, *quietly.* I have medals for diction. I can talk plenty loud.

CM 1. Will you talk a little louder?

MR. ROBESON, *loudly.* I invoke the Fifth Amendment—loudly!

INVESTIGATOR. Do you know a woman by the name of Louise Bransten?

MR. ROBESON. I invoke the Fifth Amendment.

INVESTIGATOR. I ask you to affirm or deny that on February 23, 1945, you attended a meeting in the home of Louise

144

Bransten, at which were present Max Yergan, Frederick Thompson, David Jenkins, Nancy Pittman, Dr. Lena Halpern, and Larry Fanning.

MR. ROBESON. I invoke the Fifth Amendment.

INVESTIGATOR. Do you know any of those individuals?

MR. ROBESON. I invoke the Fifth Amendment.

INVESTIGATOR. Who are Mr. and Mrs. Vladimir P. Mikheev? Do you know them?

MR. ROBESON. I have not the slightest idea, but I invoke the Fifth Amendment.

INVESTIGATOR. Mr. Chairman, the witness does not have the slightest idea who they are. I respectfully suggest he be directed to answer that question.

THE CHAIRMAN. You are directed to answer the question.

MR. ROBESON. I answer the question by invoking the Fifth Amendment.

INVESTIGATOR. Have you ever had contact with a man by the name of Gregory Kheifets?

MR. ROBESON. I invoke the Fifth Amendment.

INVESTIGATOR. Gregory Kheifets is identified with the Soviet espionage operations, is he not?

MR. ROBESON. Oh, gentlemen, I thought I was here about some passports.

INVESTIGATOR. We will get into that in just a few moments.

MR. ROBESON. This is complete nonsense.

INVESTIGATOR. Tell us whether or not you have had contact *and operations* with Gregory Kheifets.

MR. ROBESON. I invoke the Fifth Amendment.

INVESTIGATOR. Do you know a Manning Johnson?

MR. ROBESON. Manning Johnson? I only have read in the papers that he said that Dr. Ralph Bunche was some kind of fellow. He was dismissed from the FBI. He must be a pretty low character when he could be dismissed from that.

CM 1. Whether he is a low character or not, do you know him?

MR. ROBESON. I invoke the Fifth Amendment.

INVESTIGATOR. I would like to read you now some testimony, under oath before this Committee, of Manning Johnson: "In the Negro Commission of the National Committee of the Communist Party, we were told, under threat of expulsion, never to reveal that Paul Robeson was a member of the Communist Party because his assignment was confidential and secret."

MR. ROBESON. Could I protest the reading of this? If you want Mr. Manning Johnson here for cross-examination, O.K.

INVESTIGATOR. Tell us whether or not Manning Johnson was lying.

MR. ROBESON. I invoke the Fifth Amendment.

INVESTIGATOR. Have you ever been chairman of the Council on African Affairs?

MR. ROBESON. I invoke the Fifth Amendment.

INVESTIGATOR. I lay before you now a document entitled "For Freedom and Peace, Address by Paul Robeson, at Welcome Home Rally, in New York, June 19, 1949," with a photograph on it.

MR. ROBESON. I have a copy myself.

INVESTIGATOR. If you would look on the back of that pamphlet you will see "Paul Robeson, Chairman of the Council on African Affairs." Tell us whether or not you are the Paul Robeson alluded to in this document?

MR. ROBESON. I would be the Paul Robeson.

INVESTIGATOR. Then you are or have been chairman of the Council on African Affairs?

MR. ROBESON. I invoke the Fifth Amendment.

INVESTIGATOR. Do you know Max Yergan?

MR. ROBESON. I invoke the Fifth Amendment.

146

INVESTIGATOR. Max Yergan took an oath—

MR. ROBESON. Why don't you have these people here to be cross-examined? Could I ask whether this is legal?

THE CHAIRMAN. This is not only legal but usual. By a unanimous vote, this Committee has been instructed to perform this very distasteful task.

MR. ROBESON. To whom am I talking?

THE CHAIRMAN. You are speaking to the Chairman of this Committee.

MR. ROBESON. Mr. Walter?

THE CHAIRMAN. Yes.

MR. ROBESON. The Pennsylvania Walter?

THE CHAIRMAN. That is right.

MR. ROBESON. Representative of the steelworkers?

THE CHAIRMAN. That is right.

MR. ROBESON. Of the coal-mining workers? Not United States Steel, by any chance? A great patriot.

THE CHAIRMAN. That is right.

MR. ROBESON. You are the author of the bills that are going to keep all kinds of decent people out of the country.

THE CHAIRMAN. No, only your kind.

MR. ROBESON. Colored people like myself. And just the Teutonic Anglo-Saxon stock you would let come in.

THE CHAIRMAN. We are trying to make it easier to *get rid* of your kind, too!

MR. ROBESON. You don't want any colored people to come in?

Pause.

THE CHAIRMAN. Proceed.

INVESTIGATOR. Dr. Max Yergan testified: "There was a Communist core within the Council on African Affairs." Was there a Communist core?

MR. ROBESON. I will take the Fifth Amendment. Could I be allowed to read from my own statement here?

INVESTIGATOR. Will you just tell this Committee, while under oath, Mr. Robeson, the Communist who participated in the preparation of that statement?

MR. ROBESON. Oh, please.

INVESTIGATOR, *reading.* "The Chairman: Could you identify that core clearly? Of whom did it consist?"

MR. ROBESON. Could I read my statement?

INVESTIGATOR. As soon as you tell the Committee the Communists who participated in the preparation.

Pause.

Reading. "Dr. Yergan: Paul Robeson was chairman of the council and a part of that Communist-led core." Now, tell this Committee, while you are under oath, was Dr. Yergan *lying?*

MR. ROBESON. I invoke the Fifth Amendment. The reason I am here today, from the mouth of the State Department itself, is: I should not be allowed to travel because I have struggled for the independence of the colonial peoples of Africa. For many years I have so labored, and I can say modestly that my name is very much honored all over Africa. That is the kind of independence Sukarno got in Indonesia. Unless we are double-talking, these efforts in the interest of Africa would be in the same context. The other reason I am here today, again from the State Department and from the record of the court of appeals, is that when I am abroad I speak out against injustices against the Negro people of this land. That is why I am here. I am not being tried for whether I am a Communist, I am being tried for fighting for the rights of my people, who are still second-class citizens in this United States of America. My mother was born in your state, Mr. Walter, and my mother was a Quaker, and my ancestors in the time of Washington baked bread for George

Washington's troops when they crossed the Delaware. My own father was a slave. I stand here struggling for the rights of my people to be full citizens in this country. And they are not. They are not in Mississippi. And they are not in Montgomery, Alabama. And they are not in Washington. They are nowhere, and that is why I am here today. You want to shut up every Negro who has the courage to stand up and fight for the rights of his people, for the rights of workers, and I have been on many a picket line for the steelworkers too. And *that* is why I am here today.

THE CHAIRMAN. Now just a minute.

MR. ROBESON. All of this is nonsense!

THE CHAIRMAN. You ought to read Jackie Robinson's testimony.

MR. ROBESON. I know Jackie Robinson, and I am sure that in his heart he would take back a lot of what he said about me. I was one of the last people, Mr. Walter, to speak to Judge Landis, to see that Jackie Robinson had a chance to play baseball. Get the pictures and get the record. I was taken by Landis by the hand, and I addressed the combined owners of the American and the National Leagues, pleading for Robinson to be able to play baseball, like I played professional football.

INVESTIGATOR. Would you tell us whether or not you know Thomas W. Young?

MR. ROBESON. I invoke the Fifth Amendment.

INVESTIGATOR. Thomas W. Young is Negro president of the Guide Publishing Company, publishers of the *Journal and Guide* in Virginia and North Carolina. I would like to read you his testimony: "Paul Robeson has no moral right to place in jeopardy the welfare of the American Negro to advance a foreign cause in which we have no real interest. In the eyes of the Negro people this false prophet is regarded as unfaithful to their country, and they repudiate him." Do you know the man who said that?

MR. ROBESON. I invoke the Fifth Amendment. May I now read from other Negro periodicals, one of which says "Paul Robeson, Negro American," and may I read from where I am a doctor of humanities from Morehouse College, and may I read from a statement by Marshall Field, when I received the Spingarn medal from the NAACP?

THE CHAIRMAN. No.

MR. ROBESON. Why not? You allowed the other statements.

THE CHAIRMAN. This was a question, Mr. Robeson.

MR. ROBESON. I have answered the question. I take the Fifth Amendment. Now would you give me a chance to read my statement?

CM 2. Would you mind reading some of the citations you have received from Stalin?

MR. ROBESON. I have not received *any* citations from Stalin.

THE CHAIRMAN. From the Russian government?

MR. ROBESON. No. I received citations and medals from the Abraham Lincoln High School, and medals from the NAACP, and medals from many parts of the world, for my efforts for peace. Are you for war, Mr. Walter? Would you be in the category of this former Representative who felt we should have fought on the side of Hitler? *Silence.* Now can I read my statement?

CM 2. Were you in the service?

MR. ROBESON, *beginning to read the statement.* "It is a sad and bitter commentary—"

THE CHAIRMAN. Just answer the question.

INVESTIGATOR. Did you make a trip in 1949?

MR. ROBESON. Yes. I did a concert tour in England and Denmark and Sweden, and I sang for the Soviet people, one of the finest musical audiences in the world.

THE CHAIRMAN. We know all of that.

INVESTIGATOR. And while you were in Paris, did you tell an audience the American Negro would never go to war against the Soviet government?

Pause.

MR. ROBESON. Two thousand students who came from populations that would range to six or seven hundred million people asked me to say in their name that they did not want war. No part of my speech in Paris says fifteen million American Negroes would *do* anything. I said it was my feeling that the American people would struggle for peace, and that has since been underscored by President Eisenhower. Now, in passing, I said—

CM 2. Do you know *any* people who want war?

MR. ROBESON. Listen. I said it was unthinkable to me that any people would take up arms, in the name of an Eastland, against *anybody*. Gentlemen, I still say that. This United States Government should go down to Mississippi and protect my people!

INVESTIGATOR. I lay before you an article, "I Am Looking for Full Freedom," by Paul Robeson, in *The Worker,* July 3, 1949. "I said it was unthinkable that the Negro people of America or elsewhere could be drawn into war with the Soviet Union."

MR. ROBESON. I didn't say that in Paris, I said that in *The Worker.*

INVESTIGATOR, *reading.* "I repeat it with hundredfold emphasis: they will not."

MR. ROBESON. And, gentlemen, they have not done so: it is clear that no Americans, no people in the world probably, are going to war with the Soviet Union.

INVESTIGATOR. On that trip to Europe, did you go to Stockholm?

MR. ROBESON. I did. Some people in the American Embassy tried to break up my concert. They were not successful.

INVESTIGATOR. While you were in Stockholm, did you make a little speech?

MR. ROBESON. I made all kinds of speeches.

INVESTIGATOR. Let me read you a quotation.

MR. ROBESON. Let me listen.

INVESTIGATOR. Do so, please.

MR. ROBESON. I am a lawyer.

CM 2. It would be a revelation if you would listen to counsel.

MR. ROBESON. In *good* company, I usually listen. But, you know, people wander around in such fancy places. Would you please let me read my statement at some point?

THE CHAIRMAN. We will consider your statement.

INVESTIGATOR, *reading.* "I belong to the American resistance movement, which fights against American imperialism, just as the resistance movement fought against Hitler."

MR. ROBESON. Just like Frederick Douglass and Harriet Tubman were underground railroaders, and fighting for our freedom, you bet your life.

THE CHAIRMAN. I have to insist that you listen to these questions.

MR. ROBESON. I am listening.

INVESTIGATOR, *reading.* "Why should the Negroes ever fight against the only nations of the world where racial discrimination is prohibited, and where the people can live freely? Never! They will never fight against either the Soviet Union or the peoples' democracies." Did you make that statement?

MR. ROBESON. I don't remember. But what is clear is that nine hundred million other colored people have told you *they* will not. Four hundred million in India, and millions everywhere, have told you that the colored people are not going to die for anybody: they are going to die only for their independence.

CM 2. The witness has answered the question and he doesn't have to make a speech.

INVESTIGATOR. Did you go to Moscow?

MR. ROBESON. Oh, yes.

INVESTIGATOR. And while you were there, did you make a speech?

MR. ROBESON. I spoke many times and sang.

INVESTIGATOR. Did you write an article that was published in the U.S.S.R. *Information Bulletin?*

MR. ROBESON. Yes.

INVESTIGATOR, *reading.* "I want to emphasize that only here, in the Soviet Union, did I feel that I was a real man with a capital M." Did you say that?

MR. ROBESON. I would say—what is your name?

INVESTIGATOR. Arens.

MR. ROBESON. We will take this in context. I am quite willing to answer the question. When I was a singer years ago—this you have to listen to—

INVESTIGATOR. I am listening.

MR. ROBESON. I am a bass singer, and so for me it was Chaliapin, the great Russian bass, and not Caruso the tenor. I learned the Russian language to sing their songs—I wish you would *listen* now—!

CM 1. I ask you to direct the witness to answer the question.

MR. ROBESON. Just be fair to me.

CM 1. I ask regular order.

MR. ROBESON. The great poet of Russia is of African blood—

THE CHAIRMAN. Let us not go so far afield.

MR. ROBESON. It is important to explain this—

THE CHAIRMAN. Did you make that statement?

MR. ROBESON. When I first went to Russia in 1934—

THE CHAIRMAN. Did you make that statement?

MR. ROBESON. When I first went to Russia in 1934—

THE CHAIRMAN. Did you make that statement?

CM 1. I ask you to direct the witness to answer that question.

THE CHAIRMAN. Did you make that statement?

MR. ROBESON. In Russia I felt for the first time like a full human being. No color prejudice like in Mississippi, no color prejudice like in Washington. It was the first time I felt like a human being. Where I did not feel the pressure of color as I feel it in this Committee today.

CM 1. Why do you not stay in Russia?

MR. ROBESON. Because my father was a slave, and my people died to build this country, and I am going to stay here, and have a part of it just like you. And no Fascist-minded people will drive me from it. Is that clear? I am for peace with the Soviet Union, and I am for peace with China.

CM 1. You are here because you are promoting the Communist cause.

MR. ROBESON. I am here because I am opposing the neo-Fascist cause which I see in these committees. You are like the Alien and Sedition Act! Jefferson could be sitting here, and Frederick Douglass could be sitting here, and Eugene Debs could be sitting here!

THE CHAIRMAN. Are you going to answer the questions?

MR. ROBESON. I *am* answering them.

INVESTIGATOR. I again invite your attention to this article. Speaking of your son in a Soviet school in Soviet Russia: "Here he spent three years."

MR. ROBESON. And he suffered no prejudice like he would here in Washington.

INVESTIGATOR. "Then studied in a Soviet school in London."

MR. ROBESON. That is right.

INVESTIGATOR. "And in a Soviet school in New York." Did you send your son to a Soviet School in New York City?

MR. ROBESON. He was not able to go to a Soviet School in New York City. That is a mistake.

Pause.

THE CHAIRMAN. Now, what prejudice are you talking about? You were graduated from Rutgers and you were graduated from the University of Pennsylvania. I remember seeing you play football at Lehigh.

MR. ROBESON. We beat Lehigh.

THE CHAIRMAN. And we had a lot of trouble with you.

MR. ROBESON. That is right. DeWysocki was playing in my team.

THE CHAIRMAN. There was no prejudice against you. Why did you not send your son to Rutgers?

MR. ROBESON. Just a moment. This is something I challenge very deeply: that the success of a few Negroes, including myself or Jackie Robinson can make up—and here is a study from Columbia University—for seven hundred dollars a year for thousands of Negro families in the South. My father was a slave, and I have cousins who are share-croppers. I do not see success in terms of myself. I have sacrificed hundreds of thousands of dollars for what I believe in.

INVESTIGATOR. While you were in Moscow, did you make a speech lauding Stalin?

MR. ROBESON. I don't know.

INVESTIGATOR. Did you say Stalin was a great man and had done much for all the nations of the world?

MR. ROBESON. I can't remember.

INVESTIGATOR. Have you recently changed your mind about Stalin?

MR. ROBESON. What has happened to Stalin, gentlemen, is a question for the Soviet Union, and I wouldn't argue with a representative of the people who, in building America, wasted the lives of *my* people. You are responsible, you and your forebears, for sixty to one hundred million black people dying in the slave ships and on the plantations. Don't you ask me about *anybody,* please!

INVESTIGATOR. I am glad you called our attention to that slave problem. While you were in Soviet Russia, did you ask them to show you the slave labor camps?

THE CHAIRMAN. You have been so interested in slaves, I should think you'd want to see that!

MR. ROBESON. I'm interested in the place I am, and the country that can do something about it.

INVESTIGATOR. You would not, of course, discuss with us the slave labor camps in Soviet Russia?

MR. ROBESON. Nothing could be built more on slavery than *this* society, I assure you.

INVESTIGATOR. Let me read another statement by you: "The Soviet Union is the only country where I have felt completely at ease. For myself, wife, and son, the Soviet Union is our future home."

MR. ROBESON. If it were so, we would be there. My wife is here. My son is here. We have come back.

INVESTIGATOR. Let me complete this paragraph and see if it helps explain *why* it is not your future home: "For a while, however, I would not feel right going there to live. I think I can be of the most value to it by singing its praises wherever I go."

MR. ROBESON. I was born here of the Negro people, and I am back here to help them struggle.

CM 1. Did you say what he read to you?

MR. ROBESON. I don't even know what he is reading from.

It is like the statement I was supposed to make in Paris. I thought it was healthy for Americans to consider whether Negroes should fight for people who kick them around, and when they took a vote up North they got very nervous because a lot of white Americans said, "I don't see why the hell they would." Now can I read my speech?

THE CHAIRMAN. You have *made* it without reading it. Can you tell us what Communists participated in the preparation of that speech?

MR. ROBESON. Participated in what?

INVESTIGATOR. I would invite your attention to the *Daily Worker* of June 29, 1949, with reference to a get-together with you and Ben Davis, formerly Communist Councilman in New York? Do you know Ben Davis?

MR. ROBESON. One of my dearest friends, one of the finest Americans you can imagine, born of a fine family, who went to Amherst College and was a great man.

THE CHAIRMAN. The answer is yes?

MR. ROBESON. Nothing could make me prouder than to know him.

THE CHAIRMAN. That answers the question.

INVESTIGATOR. Did I understand you to laud his patriotism?

MR. ROBESON. He is as patriotic an American as there can be, and you gentlemen are the non-patriots!

THE CHAIRMAN. Just a minute!

MR. ROBESON. *You* are the un-Americans!

THE CHAIRMAN. The hearing is now adjourned!

MR. ROBESON. I should think it would be.

THE CHAIRMAN. I have endured all of this that I can.

MR. ROBESON. Can I read my statement?

THE CHAIRMAN. No. The meeting is adjourned.

MR. ROBESON. It should be. You should adjourn this forever!

157

After two more years of waiting and struggle, Paul Robeson got his passport. By that time—1958—a whole profession had been taken care of, divided and ruled, brought to heel. Some had died by their own hand, others of heart failure, many were blacklisted, many maintained their position—or improved it—by fake repentance. The investigation of show business was complete.

The Korean War had been carried through; the Vietnam War prepared for. Throughout the fifties and early sixties, resistance was minimal, so many of those who had been told to be good American had become—good Germans. Others had not, but kept alive the spirit of resistance when it was almost extinguished by men who knew what they were doing.

In 1787 Thomas Jefferson wrote to William S. Smith, "What country can preserve its liberties if its rulers are not warned from time to time that this people preserve the spirit of resistance?"

Appendix

The main source for the above pages is the printed record of the Hearings as issued by the Government Printing Office. Most of the relevant passages appear in *Thirty Years of Treason,* published in 1971 by the Viking Press. The material in the headnote to the Robeson testimony is not found, however, in either of these sources. It is based on several issues of *The Hollywood Reporter* and John Cogley's *Report on Blacklisting* (1956). It was my hope to reprint here two other items on the topic: "What José Ferrer says about Robeson," by George E. Sokolsky, *New York Journal-American,* December 30, 1952, and "Mr. Ferrer and Mr. Chaplin," a *Nation* editorial of January 31, 1953. The latter follows. But permission to reprint the former was refused by King Features Syndicate.

Mr. Ferrer and Mr. Chaplin

The Fox West Coast theater chain has canceled a scheduled opening of Charles Chaplin's "Limelight" in response to a threat by the American Legion to picket the film. Since "Limelight" has been showing for three months in New York and other cities and is not in any sense a "political" film, the Legion's action appears to be aimed not at the film but at Charles Chaplin. It is an attempt to force Mr. Chaplin to say and do certain things that the Legion wants him to do and say.

A brief review of the related case of José Ferrer will clarify matters. On December 27 the Legion announced from Hollywood that it "disapproved" of Ferrer's film "Moulin Rouge." This was after the picture's West Coast première had been picketed by nine legionnaires, most of them members of the un-American Activities Committee of the Legion's 17th District. Mr. Ferrer then wired the Legion's National Commander that he would be glad to join in the veterans' "fight against communism." A few days later Mr. Ferrer issued a statement denouncing Paul Robeson for having accepted the Stalin peace prize. On January 2 Leonard Lyons printed this interesting item in his column: "As a result of José Ferrer's anti-Red statements, the American Legion opposes any picketing of 'Moulin Rouge,' and Victor Lasky has withdrawn his Ferrer article written for the Legion magazine." On January 16 Mr. Lyons announced that Ferrer had "ironed out all his problems with the American Legion at a St. Regis luncheon with three Legion officials."

Mr. Ferrer knuckled under and the Legion's pickets were removed; Mr. Chaplin did not and his film will be picketed. This is not censorship; it is political terrorism. It has, of course, a disastrous effect on American films. "Hollywood," said Mr. Chaplin from London, "has succumbed to thought control and the illegal methods of high-pressure groups, which means the end of the American motion-picture industry and its world influence. I am afraid Hollywood is going to need me long before I need Hollywood." We agree.

72 73 74 75   12 11 10 9 8 7 6 5 4 3 2 1